A Corner to Learn

Neil Griffiths

Stanley Thornes (Publishers) Ltd

Contents

Introduction

The importance of play in the primary school classroom

It is fascinating to watch young children absorbed in play. When children are unaware of the inquisitive adult spectator, their inhibitions lift and they enter a world of make-believe, pretend and invention. Through their play, children act out imaginary roles, imitate real-life scenes and encounter new, previously unvisited situations.

Such play is crucial to the young child, as it provides many of the experiences and interaction necessary for the child's healthy intellectual, physical, emotional and social development. It allows the child freedom to explore and make sense of his or her ever-changing world, to solve problems, to set new challenges and to follow his or her natural curiosity.

The benefits of play extend well beyond early childhood and a significant contribution is made to all areas of the curriculum at both Key Stage 1 and Key Stage 2 if play is an integral part of a child's planned learning programme.

The provision and planning of play environments

Play is most successful when children are provided with good, effective stimuli. It is therefore the task of the teacher to create rich places that encourage play. Classrooms are naturally busy places and space can be limited. However, the inclusion of a quality learning corner for play is essential. When planning a play corner, careful consideration should be given to:
- the appropriateness of its theme to the children's ages and stages of development;
- the opportunities it can provide for cross-curricular learning and the development of skills throughout the National Curriculum;
- the contribution it can make to a child's language development;
- the provision it offers for social, physical and emotional development;
- the issues of gender and cultural diversity.

If children are to feel valued and to feel they have ownership of play areas, they should be heavily involved in the decision-making process of the chosen theme. Their ideas will often be more appropriate and child-centred then those imposed by adults, and will reflect their current interests and natural enthusiasm.

An important stage of the planning process will be the focus on language development. Play provides a natural context and purpose for literacy experiences and offers significant opportunities for speaking, listening, reading and writing. The learning area itself and the planned structural play opportunities should both aim to maximise the child's exposure to oral and written language. Therefore through letters, lists, posters, announcements, tape recordings and many other activities, language should remain as a central learning experience.

Introduction

Constructing a play corner

It is not necessary to be an expert in design and construction to create an imaginative play environment. However, every use should be made of talented individuals among the staff and parents who may be willing to offer their creative skills and technical knowledge.

Throughout this book the aim is to demonstrate that simple, inexpensive wooden structures can be used to provide a framework for a variety of play corner designs. These frames are easily constructed, they are adaptable and they can be 'recycled' for future use. Sturdy card (available free as discarded packaging from most retailers) or light-weight wooden sheeting is used for front, side and rear panelling. Alternatively, 'chicken-wire' covered in papier mâché is highly effective for less geometric-shaped constructions.

Again, it is most important to involve children in both the design and construction stages of the play area. The children will readily offer ideas and greatly enjoy making props and accessories. Their involvement will ensure that real ownership is given to the classroom play corner. There are further hints on play corner construction on page 78.

Props and accessories

Careful thought should be given to the choice and range of resources included in each play corner. As these resources will provide much of the 'hands-on' tactile experiences, their quality will contribute significantly to the level of much of the children's play. If the resources are well-made, varied and well-chosen, they will stimulate rich and imaginative role-play and interaction.

Consider the following points when planning props and accessories for play:
- involve children in the decision-making process;
- provide a wide range of resources that are durable and well-made;
- do not provide too many accessories as children can be overwhelmed by a large number of things to choose from;
- introduce and remove resources regularly to offer new stimuli and challenges;
- ensure resources are cared for and tidied away appropriately after use;
- offer a balance of home-made and commercially produced props;
- be aware of health and safety issues, making sure that all resources are safe and clean to use.

It is important to give children the freedom to be inventive, so not all resources need to be authentic or lifelike. Hours of pleasure can be gained from a toilet roll telescope, a yoghurt pot goblet or a washing-up liquid bottle laser gun!

All children adore dressing up and every play corner should have a supply of clothes and hats. Lavishly authentic costumes are not necessary as the children's own vivid imaginations and creativity will transform a sheet into a prince's cloak and a second-hand shoe into Cinderella's slipper!

Free and structured play

The construction and eventual completion of a classroom play corner will arouse great excitement in children. They will be eager to explore the area, dress up and begin to play with the props and accessories. But it is important that children are allowed enough time to familiarise themselves with the environment and the resources available to them.

Routines must be established and certain questions answered:
- when can the corner be used?
- how many children can play in the corner at one time?
- what resources are available and where should they be put away after use?
- how long can children play in the corner?
- what standards of behaviour are expected?

Early play experiences in the play area should be free and uninterrupted, allowing children to develop and create roles, explore boundaries, experiment with props and generally try things out (just as adults do with new gadgets at home!).

Children should be given opportunities to play alone and in groups, and adult intervention at this stage should be minimal.

However, if play is to be extended to become a rich learning experience, it is necessary to offer structure. Although children are naturally playful and can amuse themselves contentedly for hours, such play can easily become repetitive, low-level and superficial. By providing structure, you pose fresh challenges, add stimulus and offer new experiences.

Structure can be given by:
• suggesting scenarios;
• creating and adding characters;
• introducing new resources or limiting the use of existing props;
• setting specific challenges, e.g. follow a set of instructions, or act out a given story;
• restricting the use of space.

The role of the teacher in supporting the purpose of the play is highly important at this stage. A balance should be achieved between imposing adult ideas and giving children the freedom to use their own imagination. Adults should not feel inhibited about participating in the playing. Nothing will delight children more than seeing an adult join in, adopt a role and become part of their world of play.

Above, all, learning corners need to be rich, child-centred environments that stimulate imaginative play and provide wide experiences to extend children's skills and knowledge.

It is hoped that this book will be a source of inspiration to those committed to providing such rich provision for play.

Home corners

Introduction

'There's no place like home' is certainly true for young children. Home is usually a place where children feel secure and where they look forward to returning at the end of the day. The home represents the family and familiar surroundings that are central to children's busy lives.

Domestic play provides children with opportunities to make sense of their developing world and begin to understand relationships with the people around them. It will also help children learn daily routines and so establish their place among family and friends. Through structured situations in a 'home-life' environment, children will learn important life skills. During their free play they will begin to solve some of the intriguing problems that face them and experience the joys of being part of a family.

Construction

Home corners come in as many shapes and sizes as houses themselves. Homes can be bungalows, flats, bedsits, detached and semi-detached houses, cottages and town houses. They can be big or small, old or new, and made of a variety of materials.

Home for some is a palace, a lighthouse, a boat, a caravan, an hotel or a farm. Others in faraway lands live in tents, igloos, mud huts, caves and temporary shelters.

Whichever home is chosen, it will provoke some familiar issues which run through all home play, together with unique challenges that the particular style of home offers.

Settings

It is not always necessary to build an entire home - an untidy bedroom, a cluttered attic or a busy kitchen can stimulate rich play by themselves. Settings could be: bedroom, bathroom, lounge, dining room, attic, conservatory, laundry area, study, nursery, cellar, patio, garden, garage or play room.

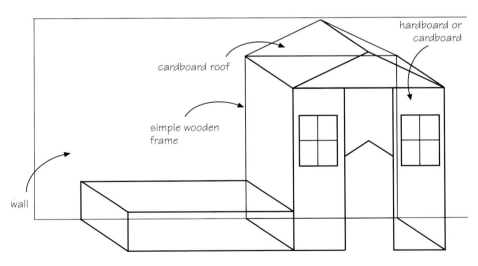

hardboard or cardboard

cardboard roof

simple wooden frame

wall

House and garden

Possible characters

Mum, dad, brothers, sisters, baby, pets, aunties, uncles, grandparents, vicar, burglar, sales person, paperboy/girl, postman/woman, firefighter, milkman/woman, gas meter reader, gardener, police officer, friends, doctor

Home corners

Props and accessories

It is important to provide an adequate stimulus for play, but many home corners become cluttered and are overwhelming in the choices they offer children. A few well-chosen items of furniture and household equipment will easily stimulate effective play.

These could include: sofa, paintings, vase, lightshade, cooker, sink (with drying rack), dining table, cutlery, pots and pans, tea set, fruit bowl, stools for table, bed, curtains, ornaments, cupboard, tablecloth, broom, iron, shopping list board, vacuum cleaner, clock, fridge, microwave oven, TV, telephone, spice rack, toaster, notice board, family photographs, baby bath, cushions, kitchen timer, magazines, first aid kit, hot-water bottles, waste bins, kitchen utensils, ironing board, flowers, washing-up liquid.

Structured play opportunities

Here are a few suggestions to direct structured play:

- a garden picnic
- washday
- bathtime
- spring cleaning
- illness in the family
- a fire
- a family argument
- an electrician calls
- the power cut
- first thing in the morning
- cooking for a special occasion
- going/returning from shopping
- family life
- going on holiday
- the burglary
- a special visitor
- a birthday
- house for sale
- last thing at night
- a rainy day indoors
- a sales person calls
- looking for something lost
- relatives come to stay

- playing at home
- a tea party
- bedtime stories
- a new baby arrives
- the wedding day
- a christening
- midnight feast
- Christmas Day

Language development

- shopping lists • newspapers • messages
- telephoning someone • labels • directions
- recipes • directories • making an audio tape of an answering machine message • bills • catalogues
- TV and radio guide • notes to family members
- prescriptions • scrapbooks • address books
- instructions for kitchen gadgets
- taping a pretend telephone conversation

Restaurant/café

Introduction

Well-known restaurants such as McDonald's and Pizza Hut are instantly appealing to young children, who get a great thrill from seeing them 'appear' in their own classroom. Children will already be familiar with many of the interior and exterior features of these restaurants and their play will quickly become realistic, reducing the need for extensive background research. A learning corner of this type is particularly effective for developing a child's social skills through the playing out of everyday situations that naturally occur in a busy eating place.

Setting up your play corner

The main structure of the restaurant is a fairly simple, light-weight, rectangular wooden frame with a cardboard canopy and thin wooden side panel (see photograph right).

Classroom items and existing home corner furniture can quickly be adapted by adding suitable motifs (temporarily attached so that they can be removed later) and by developing an appropriate colour scheme.

Tables, chairs and a cupboard can be covered in tacked-on fabric. Poster paper can be used to cover surfaces, with tacky-back plastic for protection. White paper plates and cups can easily be colour co-ordinated to match your scheme.

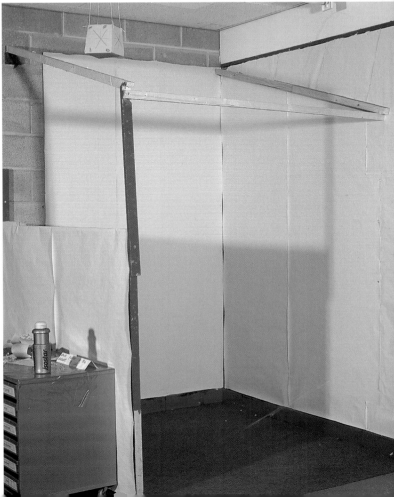

Props and accessories

Restaurants and cafés are often very generous in donating accessories for teachers to use in their classroom play activities. Although these will reduce the workload of producing props, there is still scope for a variety of home-made items.

Suggestions are: till, money, safe, cutlery, plates, cups and straws, polystyrene food containers, menus and a price list, food carrier bags, pretend food, napkins and place mats, staff notice board, opening times sign, cookers and fryers, grill pans, cleaner's polishing mop, brush and dustpan, chairs and tables, counter till receipts, order pads and pens, washing-up bowl, drying cloths, adverts, free children's gifts, special party hats, customer notices, goody bags or boxes, birthday cake.

Language development

A restaurant or café provides many rich starting points for speaking, listening, reading and writing. Customers and staff speak when ordering food and people talk when eating together. Menus and information signs have to be read and there will be opportunities for writing in many different formats. When used well, the management of a classroom restaurant or café can give a real purpose to children's language work.

• menus • order forms • till receipts • stock taking
• advert/customer evaluation forms • health and safety reports • cooking instructions • cleaning and job rotas • bank statements • party invitations
• children's complimentary quiz packs • letters of complaint • letters of thanks • staff notice board
• job descriptions • safety posters • promotional posters • adverts • accounts, bills and invoices
• job applications • audio-taped announcements to customers

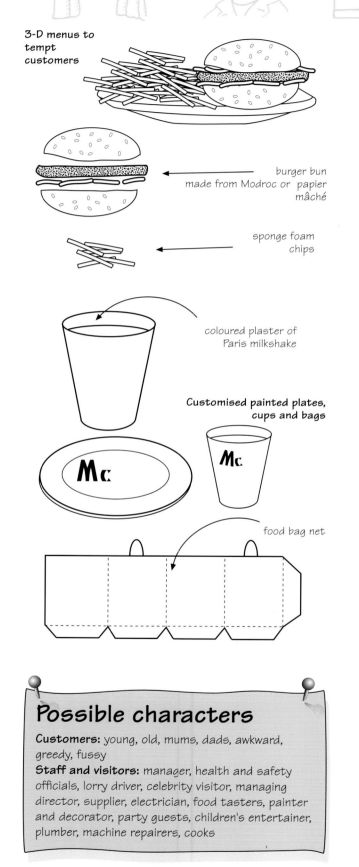

3-D menus to tempt customers

burger bun made from Modroc or papier mâché

sponge foam chips

coloured plaster of Paris milkshake

Customised painted plates, cups and bags

food bag net

Possible characters

Customers: young, old, mums, dads, awkward, greedy, fussy

Staff and visitors: manager, health and safety officials, lorry driver, celebrity visitor, managing director, supplier, electrician, food tasters, painter and decorator, party guests, children's entertainer, plumber, machine repairers, cooks

Restaurant/café

Structured play opportunities

- a children's party
- the Health Inspector's visit
- power failure or machine breakdown
- food poisoning outbreak
- customer complaints
- closed for redecoration
- promotional day
- the opening day
- a famous person visits
- food delivery
- spring cleaning
- the Managing Director arrives
- staff shortages
- a water leak

Specialised vocabulary

Food items e.g. burger, nugget, milkshake, French fries, bun

Cooking words e.g. fry, grill, microwave

Cleaning words e.g. scrub, scour, brush, polish, wipe

Restaurant vocabulary e.g. order, receipt, take-away, 'eat-in' customer, staff, manager

Menu words e.g. dessert, starter, appetiser, beverages

Utensils for cooking and cleaning e.g. spatula, knife, whisk, mop, bucket

Fun phrases e.g. Have a nice day! Can I take your order? May I help you?

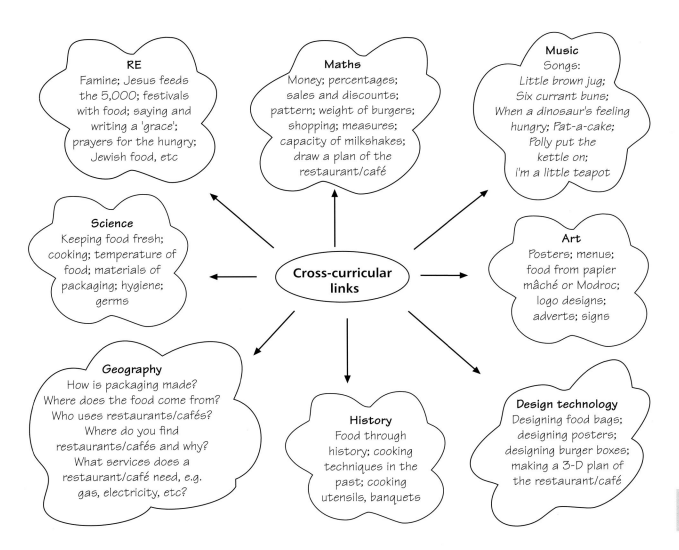

RE
Famine; Jesus feeds the 5,000; festivals with food; saying and writing a 'grace'; prayers for the hungry; Jewish food, etc

Maths
Money; percentages; sales and discounts; pattern; weight of burgers; shopping; measures; capacity of milkshakes; draw a plan of the restaurant/café

Music
Songs:
Little brown jug;
Six currant buns;
When a dinosaur's feeling hungry; Pat-a-cake;
Polly put the kettle on;
I'm a little teapot

Science
Keeping food fresh; cooking; temperature of food; materials of packaging; hygiene; germs

Cross-curricular links

Art
Posters; menus; food from papier mâché or Modroc; logo designs; adverts; signs

Geography
How is packaging made? Where does the food come from? Who uses restaurants/cafés? Where do you find restaurants/cafés and why? What services does a restaurant/café need, e.g. gas, electricity, etc?

History
Food through history; cooking techniques in the past; cooking utensils, banquets

Design technology
Designing food bags; designing posters; designing burger boxes; making a 3-D plan of the restaurant/café

13

Introduction

When observing young children enjoying domestic play, it is noticeable that they adore washing! Whether it's washing dolls' clothes, washing up pots in the kitchen sink or even washing themselves, young children have a fascination for water and getting things clean.

A launderette offers an ideal outlet for this fascination. Launderettes are naturally busy environments, giving scope for a wealth of rich play activities. Clothes will need to be washed, rinsed, dried, ironed, repaired, pressed, folded and packaged and there will be no shortage of eager young volunteers!

Setting up your play corner

Setting up a classroom launderette is not as challenging as it may first appear. Washing machines and tumble dryers are easily constructed from the outer packaging of domestic appliances. Stores are usually only too pleased to donate them.

Almost all the other necessary props can be brought in from home by the children. Ensure that all potential dangers are made safe. No launderette should be without real water. So water can be introduced by converting the classroom water tray into a hand washtub. Endless fun will be had with soap suds and there will be many opportunities for scientific discovery.

Props and accessories

Desk, telephone, diary, work rota, chair, cash register, address book, sewing machine, scissors, cotton reels, table, order book, three washing machines (colours, whites, delicates), dryer, a shelf for washing powders and detergents, baskets, waiting chair, magazines, clothes, pegs, washing line, change machine, money, signs ('Do not overload the machines', etc), cleaning materials (dusters/buckets), ironing board and iron.

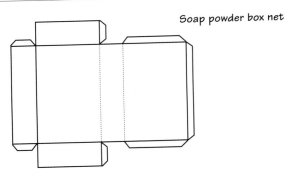

Soap powder box net

Change machine

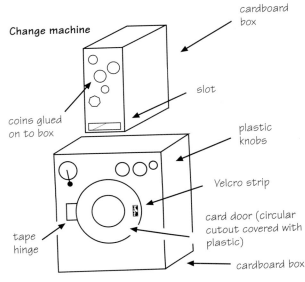

cardboard box

slot

coins glued on to box

plastic knobs

Velcro strip

card door (circular cutout covered with plastic)

tape hinge

cardboard box

Washing machine

SPECIAL

20p for a full load wash

£1 per shirt for dry cleaning

OFFER ENDS SOON

Structured play opportunities

- estimating with soap powders
- washing school football and netball kits
- sorting and classifying clothes by colour, material and size
- examining washing instruction labels
- matching up socks from an assorted basket
- the last dress!
- the ironing day
- washing for a hairdresser, a fashion designer, a restaurant, hotel or hospital
- washing disaster - an important customer's clothes shrink or turn another colour
- a flood!
- the power cut - washing by hand
- breakdowns
- the mechanic arrives
- gossip in the launderette
- stolen clothing
- repairs department - sewing, patching, etc
- washing teddies and dolls' clothes

- staff bring in an item to be washed and ironed
- removing stains with soap in a water tray
- a celebrity visits with washing
- interviewing for new staff
- washing 100 years ago with washtubs and old irons (like Mrs Tiggywinkle)
- soap suds fun in the water tray
- baskets of assorted clothes - who wears these? (children become clothing detectives)

Possible characters

Staff and visitors: receptionist, clothes repairs person, mechanic, cleaner, sales representative
Customers: celebrity, angry customer whose clothes have been ruined, football team, gossips

Language development

• writing up launderette rules • designing a safety booklet with illustrations • writing the daily activities in the diary • filling in a customer questionnaire • making name badges for employees • writing/phoning the repairs department about problems with the equipment • writing a price list for washing items • designing a special offer of the week • reading magazines while waiting for clothes to finish washing • learning telephone skills • speaking to new staff about training procedures • writing an apology letter to a customer about a ruined piece of clothing • making an audio tape of 'gossip' • making an audio tape of washing noises

Specialised vocabulary

Clothes e.g. shirt, vest, blouse, shorts
Fastenings e.g. zip, popper, Velcro
Washing words e.g. dry-clean, stain, scrub, wring, shrink, spin
Machinery e.g. dryer, change machine, washing machine
Fabrics e.g. silk, cotton, whites, coloureds
Repair words e.g. stitch, sew, hem, fray
Water words e.g soak, rinse, splash

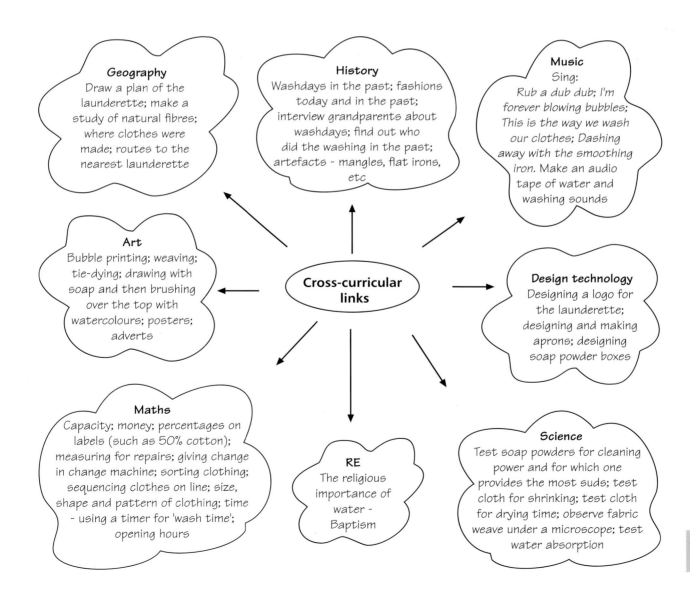

Geography
Draw a plan of the launderette; make a study of natural fibres; where clothes were made; routes to the nearest launderette

History
Washdays in the past; fashions today and in the past; interview grandparents about washdays; find out who did the washing in the past; artefacts - mangles, flat irons, etc

Music
Sing:
Rub a dub dub; I'm forever blowing bubbles; This is the way we wash our clothes; Dashing away with the smoothing iron. Make an audio tape of water and washing sounds

Art
Bubble printing; weaving; tie-dying; drawing with soap and then brushing over the top with watercolours; posters; adverts

Cross-curricular links

Design technology
Designing a logo for the launderette; designing and making aprons; designing soap powder boxes

Maths
Capacity; money; percentages on labels (such as 50% cotton); measuring for repairs; giving change in change machine; sorting clothing; sequencing clothes on line; size, shape and pattern of clothing; time - using a timer for 'wash time'; opening hours

RE
The religious importance of water - Baptism

Science
Test soap powders for cleaning power and for which one provides the most suds; test cloth for shrinking; test cloth for drying time; observe fabric weave under a microscope; test water absorption

Flower shop

Introduction

The inclusion of a flower shop will brighten up any classroom and provide a starting point for purposeful play. Young children are fascinated by the beauty and variety of flower and plant life, and the shop can make a valuable contribution towards their scientific development.

Children will be eager to bring in fresh flowers from their own gardens (if the season permits) and a visit from a real florist can be a worthwhile additional experience. There is great potential for artwork, and designing and constructing paper flowers will be enjoyed by everyone.

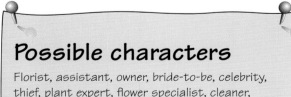

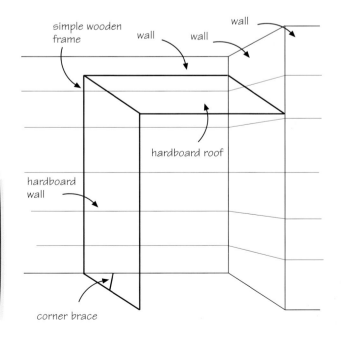

Constructing your play corner

The shop's external structure consists of a simple side support and a frame for a canopy-style roof. Internally there will be a need for shelves, a counter and containers for flowers, plants and other florist's items. The interior can then be decorated with the children's own colourful posters and signs.

Possible characters

Florist, assistant, owner, bride-to-be, celebrity, thief, plant expert, flower specialist, cleaner, customers, manager, window cleaner, delivery person, postman/woman

simple wooden frame

wall

wall

wall

hardboard roof

hardboard wall

corner brace

19

Props and accessories

A visit to any real florist's shop leaves you with the impression that every inch of space is in use. The area is always a blaze of colour, with shelves full of flora of every kind. A classroom shop should mirror this. Children will need to handle items with care and move carefully around the shop interior. There are hundreds of ways of making paper flowers and parents are often keen to come into school and help with their own ideas. Other items could be brought in from home and many florist's shops respond generously to a thoughtful letter of request.

Props could include: ribbons, Oasis, dried flowers, paper flowers, wrapping paper, posters, adverts, buckets, plastic vases, plant sprayers, flower pots, order forms, till, money, message cards, notelets, catalogues, baskets.

Structured play opportunities

• the shop's opening day • the wedding - first the bride chooses her flowers and then it's the day of the wedding • a party/celebration - flowers for the occasion • preparing flowers for someone special • a thief breaks in • preparing for a flower arranging competition • Mother's Day • the annual flower show • the day of the plant sale • Valentine's Day • cleaning the shop • promotion evening • an unusual visitor - the Queen, a film star, a TV celebrity • plant and flower advice - an expert is on hand in the shop • a busy day • an angry and disappointed customer • stock-taking day • sending flowers by post or Interflora • a visit to the flower market • delivery day - supplies arrive • the phone never stops ringing! • a greenfly epidemic hits the shop • the power cut! • flower of the week • preparing window displays

Home-made flowers

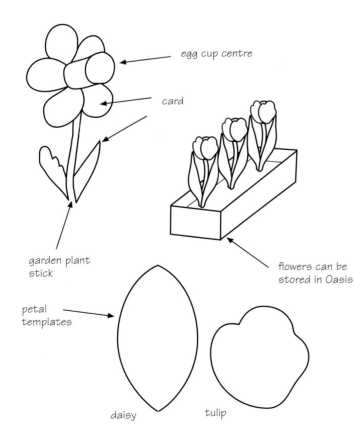

egg cup centre

card

garden plant stick

petal templates

flowers can be stored in Oasis

daisy   tulip

Home-made seed packets

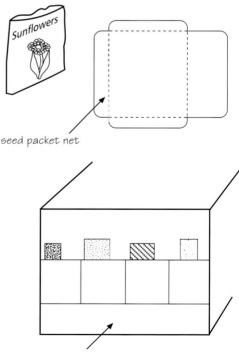

seed packet net

simple card pockets can be used to display seed packets or greetings cards

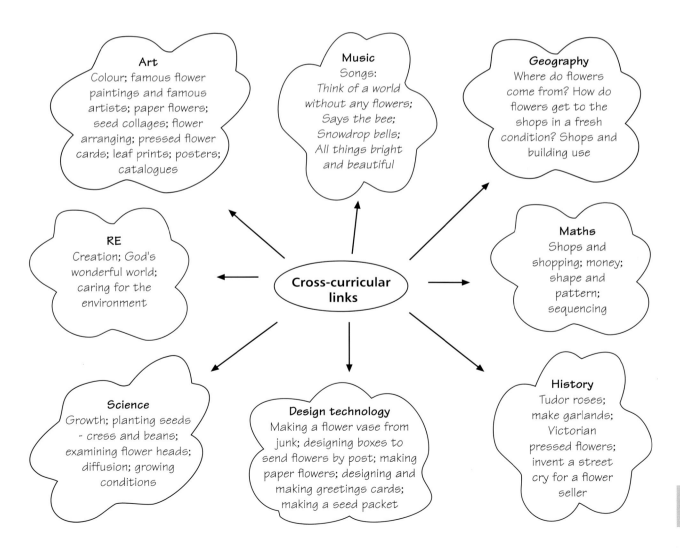

Language development

- letters of complaint, praise or requesting information
- stock-taking forms
- order forms
- invoices
- Interflora paperwork
- telephone messages
- designing catalogues
- plant care instructions
- message tags for all occasions
- labels
- price lists
- adverts
- receipts

Specialised vocabulary

Flower names *e.g. rose, orchid, pansy*
Flower parts *e.g. petal, leaf, stem*
Florist vocabulary *e.g. spray, posy, corsage, buttonhole, bouquet, wreath, basket, bunch, arrangement*
Florist items *e.g. ribbon, Oasis, Cellophane*
Shop furniture/accessories *e.g. counter, till, order form, vases, display case, pots, plant sprayer*
Occasions vocabulary *e.g. celebration, invitation, reception, Valentine*

Art
Colour; famous flower paintings and famous artists; paper flowers; seed collages; flower arranging; pressed flower cards; leaf prints; posters; catalogues

Music
Songs:
Think of a world without any flowers;
Says the bee;
Snowdrop bells;
All things bright and beautiful

Geography
Where do flowers come from? How do flowers get to the shops in a fresh condition? Shops and building use

RE
Creation; God's wonderful world; caring for the environment

Cross-curricular links

Maths
Shops and shopping; money; shape and pattern; sequencing

Science
Growth; planting seeds – cress and beans; examining flower heads; diffusion; growing conditions

Design technology
Making a flower vase from junk; designing boxes to send flowers by post; making paper flowers; designing and making greetings cards; making a seed packet

History
Tudor roses; make garlands; Victorian pressed flowers; invent a street cry for a flower seller

Maths market

Introduction

Although most learning corners are widely cross-curricular, this market stall has been specifically designed to develop maths skills. The market aims to provide mathematical learning through play, and the carefully structured props will introduce concepts and extend skills, knowledge and understanding. The activities generated encourage practical, hands-on exploration. They also provide the teacher with the opportunity to widen the children's mathematical experiences, and to stimulate talk and the use of specialised vocabulary. Above all, the market is designed to demonstrate to children that maths is fun, real and part of everyday life.

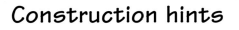 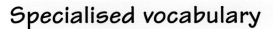

Construction hints

The market is a simple, wooden-framed design with a fabric or cardboard canopy roof. Plenty of shelving is needed for the storage and display of packages, and a small table for the till, scales and telephone.

Props and accessories

Almost all the props can be brought in from home or made by the children themselves. For hygiene reasons all food items will need to be removed from their packaging, although dried foods such as rice or pasta can remain if replaced termly.

The children will enjoy making pretend groceries from papier mâché, card, paper, Modroc or plaster of Paris. In addition, a till, money (real, if possible), telephone, notepads and receipts can be included.

Specialised vocabulary

Time *e.g. fast, slow, o'clock*
Shape *e.g. hexagon, cube, diagonal, corner*
Area *e.g. surface, length, width*
Length *e.g. long, short, centimetre*
Capacity *e.g. full, empty, pour, fill*
Weight *e.g. light, heavy, balance*
Money *e.g. sale, share, pound*
Fractions *e.g. half, quarter, eighth*
Number *e.g. add, subtract, share, multiply, tens*

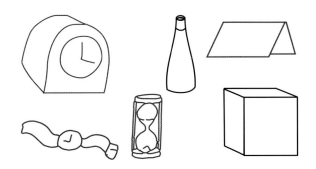

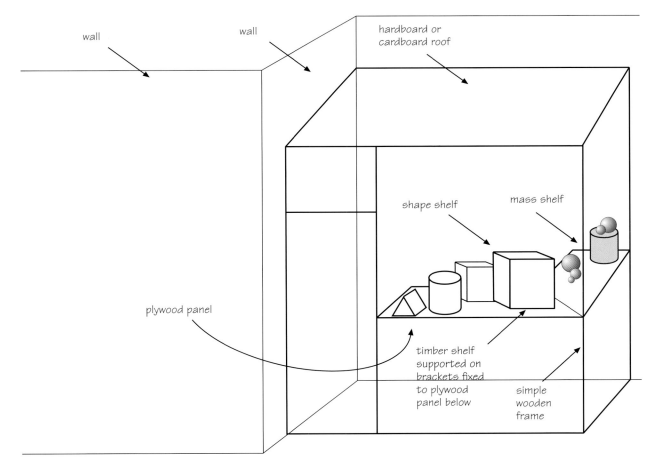

wall

wall

hardboard or cardboard roof

shape shelf

mass shelf

plywood panel

timber shelf supported on brackets fixed to plywood panel below

simple wooden frame

23

Activities

The market has been designed to represent all aspects of maths - from measures to multiplication and from sharing to shape. Each shelf is devoted to a theme, and cards suggest activities and introduce important vocabulary. Although the market can be used independently by children in their free play, it is designed for use by small groups accompanied by an adult who directs learning.

Time: clocks, sand timers, stopwatches, watches

Shape: 3-D packaging e.g. Toblerone (triangular prism), etc. The market is decorated with 2-D shapes for the children to identify.

Area: wrapping paper and greetings cards

Length: balls of string, ribbons, laces

Capacity: plastic bottles of different sizes– full, empty, half-full

Weight: packages of varying weight e.g. rice, pasta, dog biscuits

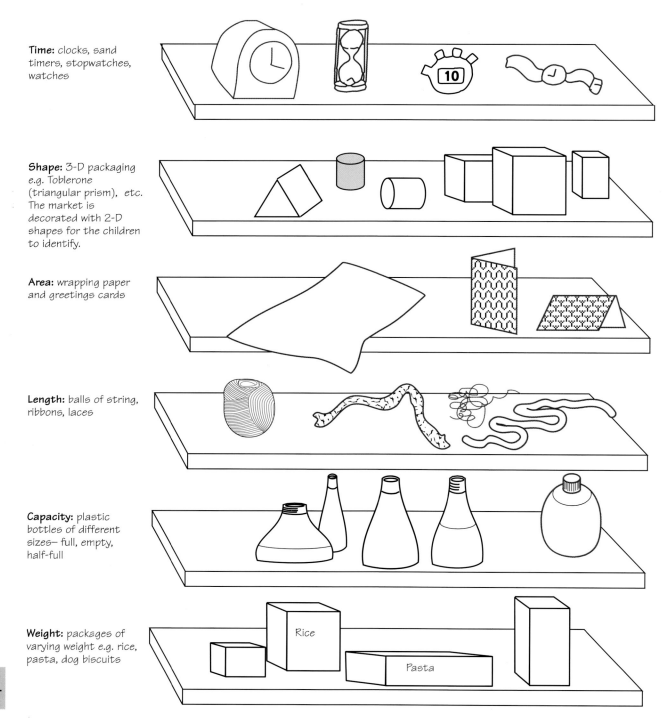

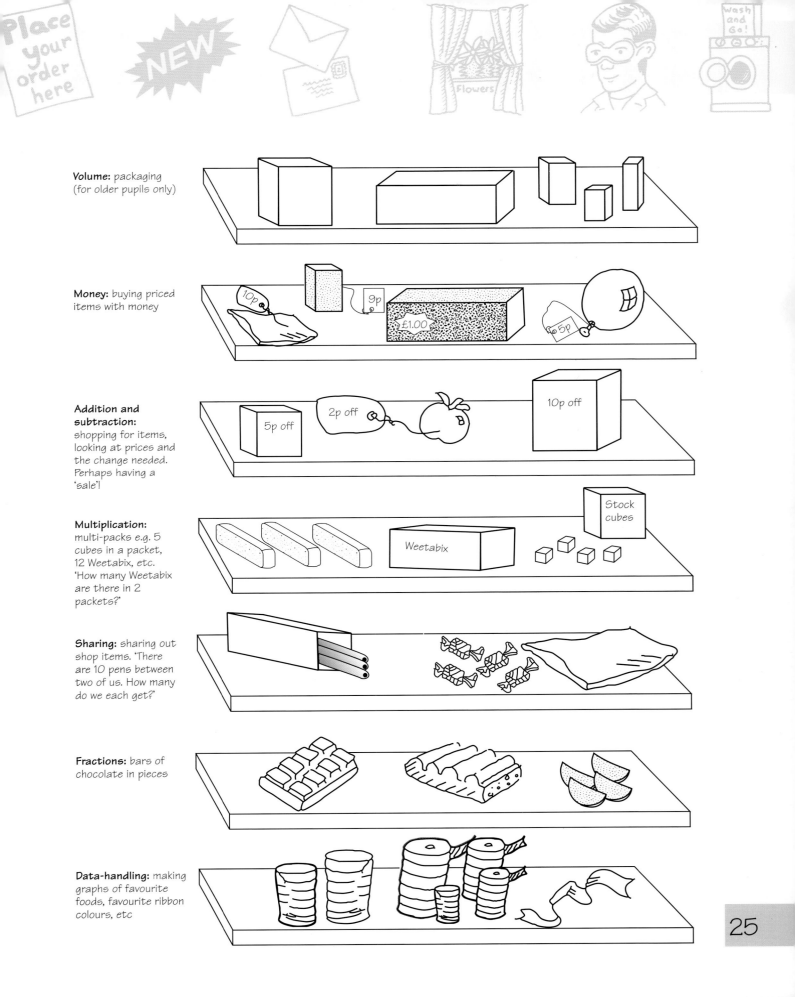

Volume: packaging (for older pupils only)

Money: buying priced items with money

10p

9p

£1.00

5p

Addition and subtraction: shopping for items, looking at prices and the change needed. Perhaps having a 'sale'!

5p off

2p off

10p off

Multiplication: multi-packs e.g. 5 cubes in a packet, 12 Weetabix, etc. 'How many Weetabix are there in 2 packets?'

Weetabix

Stock cubes

Sharing: sharing out shop items. 'There are 10 pens between two of us. How many do we each get?'

Fractions: bars of chocolate in pieces

Data-handling: making graphs of favourite foods, favourite ribbon colours, etc

Introduction

Children adore posting letters and opening parcels, and they are always eager to greet the postman or postwoman who calls at their house. Most children are familiar with their local or town centre post office. For younger children the postal service is often associated with greetings cards, Christmas gifts and collections of attractive stamps.

Children will quickly become absorbed in the busy environment that a post office provides and will invent unusual destinations for mail items. They will be eager to serve behind the counter or trudge imaginary streets delivering the post.

Setting up your play corner

A post office does not need to have an elaborate exterior structure - it is the contents of the interior that will dictate the quality of play provision.

A counter is a must, together with adequate space for weighing and wrapping parcels, and storage for the many forms and the large amount of paperwork that a post office generates.

No post office would be complete without a postbox. Children generally prefer the traditional free-standing postbox to the 'hole in the wall' type.

Post office

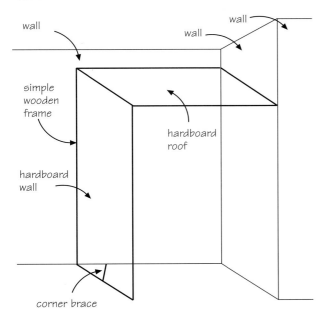

wall

wall

wall

simple wooden frame

hardboard roof

hardboard wall

corner brace

coin slots

knobs e.g. screw bottle tops

collecting tray

Stamp machine

'sick' bags or brown paper bags

card fixed to wall

Sorting bags

Sorting bag net

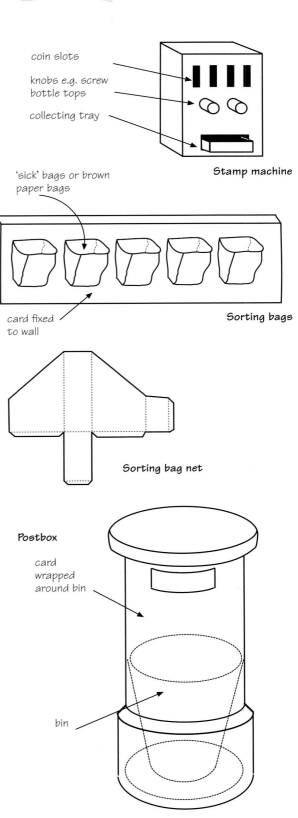

Props and accessories

Parcels of various weights, envelopes, scales, greetings cards, wrapping paper, stamps, stamp machine, stamp pad, rubber stamp, till, money, TV licence and car tax forms, telephone, pens, paper, parcel tags, post office savings books, posters, information leaflets, pension books, sorting baskets, mailbag.

Postbox

card wrapped around bin

bin

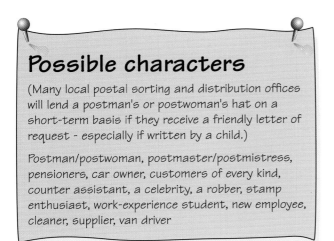

Possible characters

(Many local postal sorting and distribution offices will lend a postman's or postwoman's hat on a short-term basis if they receive a friendly letter of request – especially if written by a child.)

Postman/postwoman, postmaster/postmistress, pensioners, car owner, customers of every kind, counter assistant, a celebrity, a robber, stamp enthusiast, work-experience student, new employee, cleaner, supplier, van driver

Structured play opportunities

- an armed robbery
- weighing parcels
- collecting and delivering the post
- the lost parcel
- wrapping gifts
- stamp collectors' fair
- pension day
- sending a telemessage
- designing a new stamp
- acting out stories from *Postman Pat* and *The Jolly Postman*
- delivering to a special party
- the Christmas rush
- letters to royalty and famous people
- studying letter destinations and places of postage
- franking letters
- a celebrity visits
- spring clean
- sorting Santa's mail to Lapland

Language development

• writing/posting thank-you letters • writing to a celebrity • making TV licence and car tax forms • price lists • addressing envelopes • making and sending postcards • opening and closing times information • inventing greetings card verses • designing new stamps • luggage labels • adverts • a complaints form • a stamp brochure • reading addresses on letters brought from home • sorting and delivering the school mail

Specialised vocabulary

Address words *e.g. street, postcode, town, city, county*

Postal words *e.g. addressee, franking, parcel, air-mail*

Services *e.g. pension, TV licence, car tax, premium bond*

Resources *e.g. envelopes, greetings cards, first-day covers, labels, application forms*

Equipment *e.g. scales, rubber stamp, franking machine*

Science laboratory

Introduction

Inside many children there's a budding young scientist just bursting to be set free! Children of all ages are eager to design and carry out pretend experiments, and investigate bottles of mysteriously coloured potions and liquids. The presence of a classroom science laboratory gives children the opportunity to test with tubes, observe through microscopes and lenses, mix and pound with pestle and mortar, and heat bubbling substances with the Bunsen burner (flameless, of course!). Ideas will overflow as children act out imaginary scenes in which they discover the powers of shrinking powder and find a cure for chickenpox!

Construction hints

A rectangular wooden frame can quickly be transformed into a modern laboratory with the application of silver foil and signs warning of

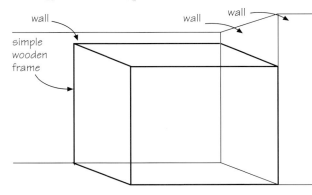

'explosive chemicals', 'danger' and 'scientists at work'! Interior shelving will be needed to display lots of bottles, jars and test tubes, and a safe box will be required to store the pretend explosive powders. A discarded vacuum cleaner hose can serve as an extractor tube and inexpensive guttering adds to the effect. A table should be provided to be used as a science bench and children can then create their own laboratory machinery, using boxes, toilet rolls and junk materials.

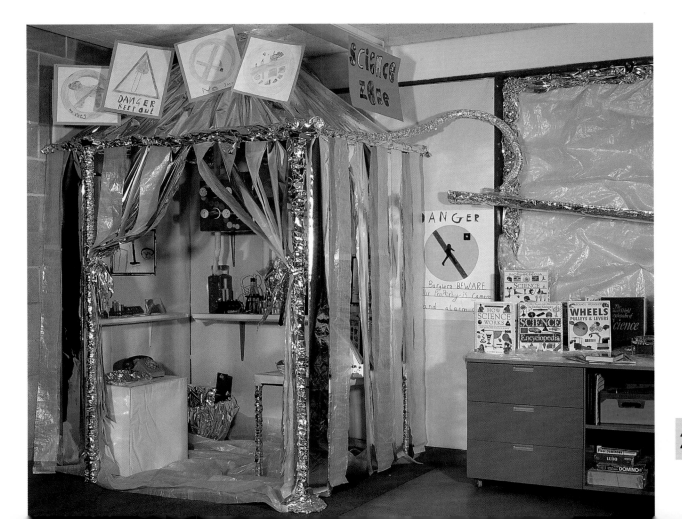

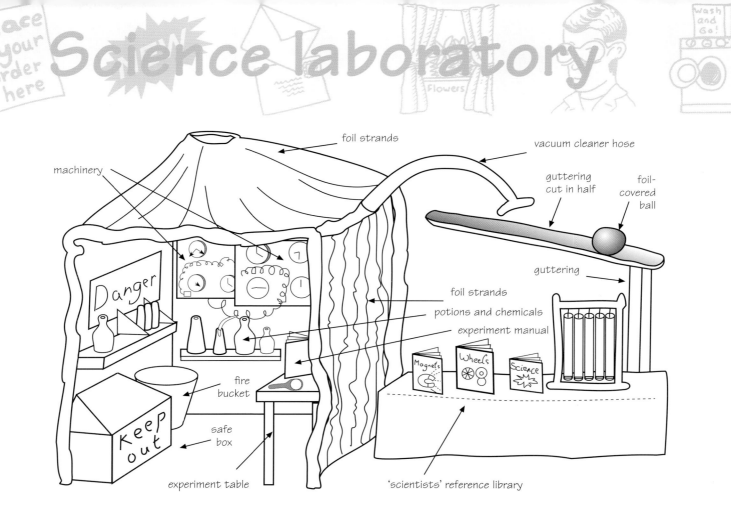

machinery

foil strands

vacuum cleaner hose

guttering cut in half

foil-covered ball

Danger

foil strands

potions and chemicals

experiment manual

guttering

Magnets

Wheels

Science

fire bucket

safe box

Keep out

experiment table

'scientists' reference library

Props and accessories

No glass items should be included in the play corner but plastic sweet jars and food containers will be adequate substitutes to hold pretend chemicals. Water can be coloured with ink or food colouring and custard powder, flour and chalk can be used for grinding and mixing. Baking powder and sherbet will also create a wonderful fizz when water is added!

Other props could include: microscope, plastic test tubes, magnifying glass, goggles, scales, stopwatch, bubble mixture and bubble blower, Bunsen burner, tongs, mixing bowls and spoons, pestle and mortar, litmus paper, clipboard, log book, specimen jars, Petri dishes, white coats, face masks, rubber gloves, first aid kit, health and safety chart, mirrors, magnets, rulers.

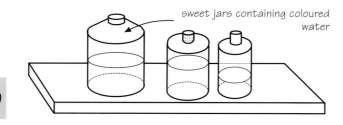

sweet jars containing coloured water

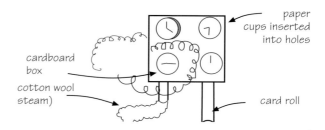

paper cups inserted into holes

cardboard box

cotton wool steam)

card roll

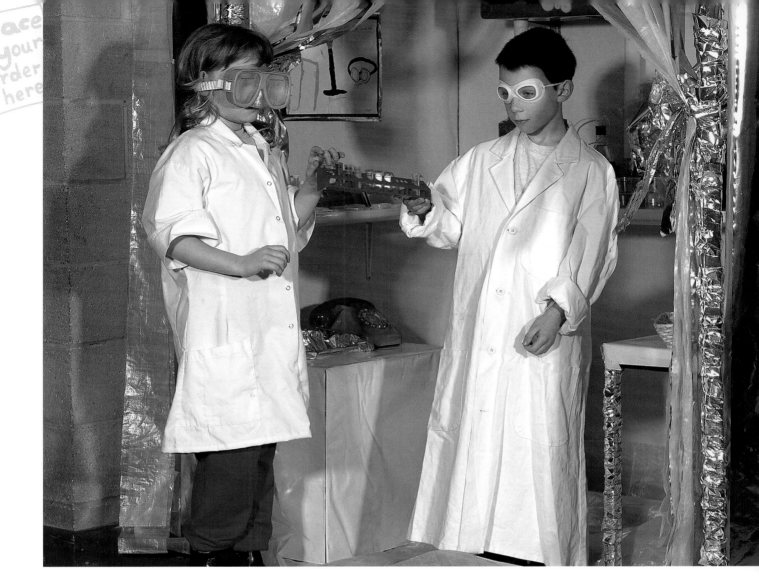

Structured play opportunities

- carrying out pretend experiments
- inventing potions
- the equipment that went wrong!
- carrying out real experiments that are safe
  (perhaps using a child's chemistry kit)
- a famous discovery
- inventing a disappearing pill!
- growing crystals
- the cure!
- magnet and electric circuit play
- using the play corner to complete real experiments
  that are part of the class's science work - growing
  cress, exploring materials, etc
- making up formulae in an experiment book
- the explosion!
- the robbery of a scientist's notebook

Language development

- writing a safety manual • warning posters •
laboratory users' guide • log books and a scientist's
diary • order forms for chemicals • writing
descriptions of experiments • making up formulae
- producing laboratory catalogues • labels
- producing an audio tape of laboratory noises
- pretending to give a science lecture to the class
- writing a 'young scientist' magazine • a coded
message for a spy who is trying to steal a formula

Specialised vocabulary

Chemicals *e.g. acid, hydrogen, copper sulphate*
Containers *e.g. jar, pestle and mortar, test tube*
Safety words *e.g. protective clothing, face mask,
safety goggles, sterilise*
Scientific words *e.g. experiment, formulae, discovery,
dissolve, heat, extinguish*
Equipment *e.g. microscope, Bunsen burner, slide*

Sea and seashore

Introduction

It can be surprising to discover how many young children have not visited the seaside, yet many class summer projects centre on the study of the sea.

By creating a beach or under-the-sea play area, you can provide children with the next-best experience and give them a valuable insight into what life is like underwater, the thrill of rock pool dipping, and how it feels to get sand between your toes!

Opportunities will arise for scientific and geographical study, together with a rich variety of creative and enjoyable craft activities.

Setting up your play corner

Teachers are often looking for meaningful ways to use sand and water in their classrooms. This play corner develops the use of both of these to the full. Simple shreds of black, grey and green bin liners acting as seaweed will instantly transform a water tray into a lifelike rock pool, while the sand tray will provide hours of beach fun with the addition of pebbles, shells, buckets, spades and sandcastle flags. Netting can be hung from the ceiling, together with card clouds and seagulls to give an authentic feel. Children can paint horizons or an underwater scene on a window. Sunlight will then create a lifelike effect. The inclusion of a lighthouse will add an extra dimension to the structured play - including stormy nights and shipwrecks.

netting

window painted with powder paint (add washing-up liquid for easy removal)

card

card

layers of tissue

water tray

sand tray

lighthouse

Lighthouse

wall

plywood top

timber uprights joining base and top

card wrapped over frame

hexagonal prism frame in balsa or softwood

perspex or polythene panels

hexagonal timber base

Sand tray

flag

plastic spade

sandcastle

Water tray

toy fish

stones

bin liner strips

Possible characters

Deck-chair attendant, tourists, family members, travel agent, deep-sea diver, lifeguard, scientist, explorer, lighthouse keeper, rubbish collector, first aider, café owner

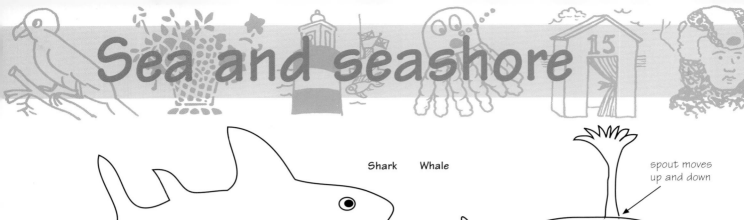

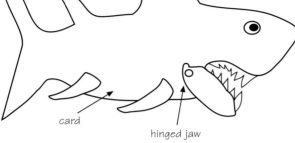

Shark   Whale

spout moves up and down

card

hinged jaw

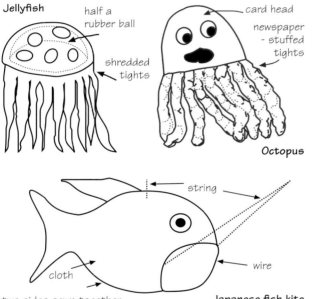

Jellyfish

half a rubber ball

card head

newspaper - stuffed tights

shredded tights

shredded tights

Octopus

string

wire

cloth

two sides sewn together

Japanese fish kite

Structured play opportunities

- preparing for a picnic - making sandwiches, etc
- getting ready to go on holiday
- undersea adventure
- finding hidden treasure
- shipwreck
- the lighthouse keeper's famous day
- sandcastle building competition
- monster from the deep
- lost at sea
- rock-pool dipping and scientific survey
- lifeguard rescue
- a family day on the beach
- washed ashore on a deserted island
- a disastrous holiday

Props and accessories

The children will adore dressing up in their latest beach/swim wear and no underwater exploration would be complete without a snorkel, goggles and flippers. Stores such as the Early Learning Centre and Toys R Us sell excellent underwater creatures for the rock pool and every household will have a collection of shells and pebbles you may be able to borrow. There are hundreds of ways of making fish and underwater creatures. Some suggestions are shown above.

Other useful props include: net, sandcastle flags, magnifying glass to look at underwater creatures, buckets, deck-chair, toy boats, spades, sand moulds.

34

Language development

• make and write postcards home • make hidden treasure maps • design and make holiday and hotel brochures • messages in a bottle • weather charts • navigation maps • surveys of fish and underwater creatures • make books of underwater information • menus of a seaside café • make an audio tape of seaside or underwater sounds • lighthouse keeper's log book • a holiday diary • a travel agent's brochure • letters home • picnic menus • read seaside stories • make a holiday checklist of things you need to take

Specialised vocabulary

Seaside words *e.g.* pier, lifeguard, sandstorm
Underwater words *e.g.* seaweed, octopus, snorkel
Water words *e.g.* wave, ripple, froth
Holiday words *e.g.* passport, travel agent, luggage
Beach words *e.g.* sandcastle, deck-chair, wind-break, donkey rides, paddle, costume, sunstroke
Geographical words *e.g.* horizon, island, sunset
Food words *e.g.* candyfloss, toffee apple, rock
Picnic words *e.g.* tablecloth, basket, cutlery

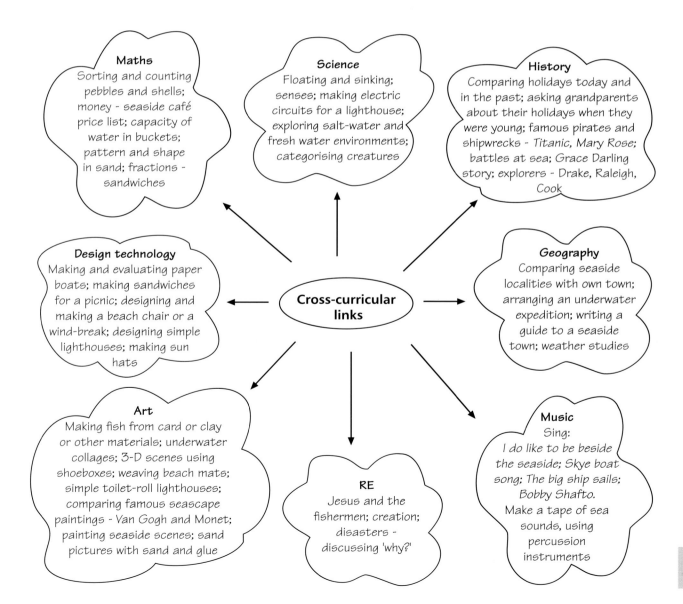

Maths
Sorting and counting pebbles and shells; money - seaside café price list; capacity of water in buckets; pattern and shape in sand; fractions - sandwiches

Science
Floating and sinking; senses; making electric circuits for a lighthouse; exploring salt-water and fresh water environments; categorising creatures

History
Comparing holidays today and in the past; asking grandparents about their holidays when they were young; famous pirates and shipwrecks - *Titanic, Mary Rose*; battles at sea; *Grace Darling* story; explorers - Drake, Raleigh, Cook

Design technology
Making and evaluating paper boats; making sandwiches for a picnic; designing and making a beach chair or a wind-break; designing simple lighthouses; making sun hats

Cross-curricular links

Geography
Comparing seaside localities with own town; arranging an underwater expedition; writing a guide to a seaside town; weather studies

Art
Making fish from card or clay or other materials; underwater collages; 3-D scenes using shoeboxes; weaving beach mats; simple toilet-roll lighthouses; comparing famous seascape paintings - Van Gogh and Monet; painting seaside scenes; sand pictures with sand and glue

RE
Jesus and the fishermen; creation; disasters - discussing 'why?'

Music
Sing:
I do like to be beside the seaside; Skye boat song; The big ship sails; Bobby Shafto.
Make a tape of sea sounds, using percussion instruments

Woodland and forest

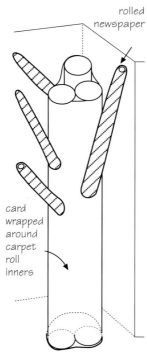

rolled newspaper

card wrapped around carpet roll inners

Introduction

A woodland scene makes a very attractive addition to any classroom and can provide excellent starting points for science activities and the development of environmental study skills. Children's play might focus on unusual plant life, a mini-beast hunt or even a fungi foray! Every sense will be active as children crunch leaves under foot, feel the rough textures of bark and smell the scent of damp earth. Through subtle variations over the duration of a term, children can experience the changing seasons as golden leaves, frosted twigs and bright summer flowers are added.

Construction hints

The most difficult aspect of designing a woodland play corner is the construction of the trees. Two methods are recommended:

1 Chicken-wire frame
This can be built in the rough shape of a trunk with boughs and branches, and then covered in a thin layer of papier mâché (see diagram right).

2 Carpet roll inners and papier mâché
Alternatively, three or four carpet roll inners can be taped together to act as a trunk. Branches made from rolled newspaper are then attached to it (see diagram above). The whole tree is covered in a thin layer of papier mâché and painted. Paper leaves can be pinned or stapled on to give a lifelike effect. If sponges are used to apply the paint to the trunk and branches, the end result is much more realistic. Fallen logs can be made using similar methods and the corner can be transformed into a woodland by adding leaves, plants, flowers, moss, mini-beasts and woodland creatures.

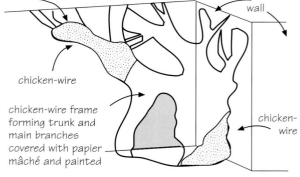

branches fixed to ceiling

wall

chicken-wire

chicken-wire frame forming trunk and main branches covered with papier mâché and painted

chicken-wire

Woodland animal

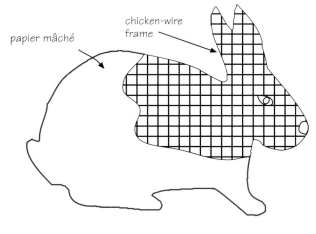

papier mâché

chicken-wire frame

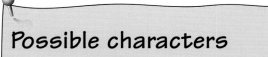

Possible characters

Park rangers, woodland explorers, Percy the park keeper, a search party, landowners, nursery rhyme and fairy tale characters such as Red Riding Hood and Goldilocks, a forester, a plant expert, a botanist, lost travellers, hunters, a lumberjack, a farmer, poachers, police

Props and accessories

Magnifying glasses, wellingtons, nets for catching bugs, lunch-box, picnic basket, pretend food, blanket, binoculars, identification book, painting easel and paints, camera, maps, torches, tape recorder, backpacks, thermometer.

A woodland lends itself to the inclusion of 'living' things. If these are cared for by the children, they will survive for some time. Here are some suggestions: moss, leaves, potted plants (disguise pots with leaves and moss), bark, conifers, acorns, soil, branches, fresh flowers (regularly replaced). Mini-beasts can also be kept for short periods in suitable containers provided that they are fed and returned to their natural habitat.

Woodland creatures can be made in lots of imaginative ways, using papier mâché, chicken-wire moulds, plaster of Paris, clay, fabric or card. The corner could include models of: birds, fungi, insects, mammals, fish in a pond, amphibians, nocturnal creatures.

Specialised vocabulary

Woodland creatures *e.g.* bumblebee, squirrel, hawk
Environmental words *e.g.* pollution, rare, protected
Woodland features *e.g.* copse, clearing, glade, clump
Plants *e.g.* buttercup, mushroom, nettle
Plant parts *e.g.* branch, twig, petal, stem, root
Seasonal words *e.g.* frosty, icicles, hibernation
Mapping words *e.g.* route, symbols, bearings
Equipment *e.g.* binoculars, compass, sample jar, thermometer

Language development

• writing a country code • warning posters • identification books • maps • making up a woodland quiz • writing directions to the woods • woodland guides • information booklets • an audio tape of woodland sounds • letters to conservation groups

Structured play opportunities

• a woodland picnic • the woods at night • lost! • the rescue party • the rare discovery • finding hidden treasure • fungi foray • bug hunt • bird spotting • animal tracking • the hunt • acting out *We're going on a bear hunt* or *Goldilocks*

• woodland survey • the magic wood • hunting for clues • meeting a leprechaun or an elf • 'save our forest' demonstration • a day out • the storm • a day painting in the woods • setting a trail for others to follow • woodland quiz night

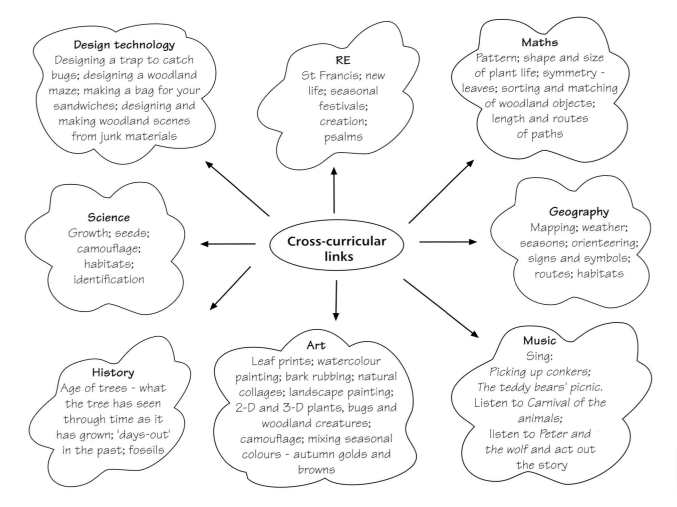

Design technology
Designing a trap to catch bugs; designing a woodland maze; making a bag for your sandwiches; designing and making woodland scenes from junk materials

RE
St Francis; new life; seasonal festivals; creation; psalms

Maths
Pattern; shape and size of plant life; symmetry - leaves; sorting and matching of woodland objects; length and routes of paths

Science
Growth; seeds; camouflage; habitats; identification

Cross-curricular links

Geography
Mapping; weather; seasons; orienteering; signs and symbols; routes; habitats

History
Age of trees - what the tree has seen through time as it has grown; 'days-out' in the past; fossils

Art
Leaf prints; watercolour painting; bark rubbing; natural collages; landscape painting; 2-D and 3-D plants, bugs and woodland creatures; camouflage; mixing seasonal colours - autumn golds and browns

Music
Sing:
*Picking up conkers;
The teddy bears' picnic.*
Listen to *Carnival of the animals;*
listen to *Peter and the wolf* and act out the story

Underground worlds

Introduction

There is a fascination for children in watching something disappear underground. It leads to endless questions and a desire to explore the unknown. Where has it gone? What is it like underground? How far can you go? A classroom mine encourages children to find answers to these and other questions about life underground.

Construction hints

A rectangular wooden frame needs to be covered in chicken-wire mesh. The whole exterior and interior will have to be coated with several layers of papier mâché to ensure no wire is left exposed. Fun can then be had in creating an authentic look with coal seams, diamond clusters and gleaming rubies. Paper-padded, coal-shaped, black polythene looks very realistic as coal but for the brave-hearted there is no substitute for the real thing - even if it is messy.

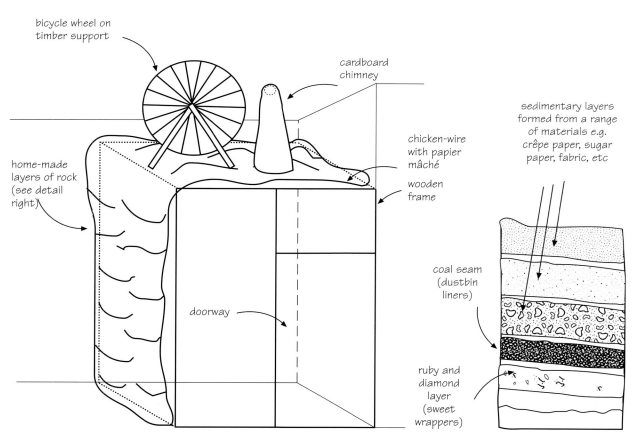

bicycle wheel on timber support

cardboard chimney

home-made layers of rock (see detail right)

chicken-wire with papier mâché

wooden frame

doorway

sedimentary layers formed from a range of materials e.g. crêpe paper, sugar paper, fabric, etc

coal seam (dustbin liners)

ruby and diamond layer (sweet wrappers)

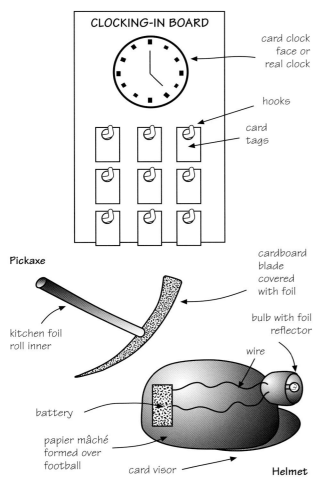

CLOCKING-IN BOARD

card clock
face or
real clock

hooks

card
tags

Pickaxe

cardboard
blade
covered
with foil

bulb with foil
reflector

wire

kitchen foil
roll inner

battery

papier mâché
formed over
football

card visor

Helmet

Structured play opportunities

- digging for gold
- trapped underground
- diamond discovery
- geological survey
- a day in the life of a miner
- a guided mine tour
- *Hi ho, Hi ho, it's off to work we go* (the seven dwarfs from the fairy tale go mining)
- the miners' strike
- journey to the centre of the Earth
- rescue party
- tunnelling to freedom
- smugglers' cave
- pit closure
- finding hidden treasure underground

Props and accessories

Pickaxe, drill, lanterns, buckets, sacks, coal, clocking-in machine, overalls, spades, first-aid kit, maps, charts, sandwich boxes, towels, helmets, soap.

Language development

- newspaper reports of mine disasters • adverts •underground maps • safety rules and procedures • miners' diaries • buried treasure maps • job application forms • machine instructions

41

Jet airliner

Introduction

The presence of an airliner in a classroom will always act as a great stimulus to children of all ages. It will immediately direct and challenge a child's imagination - evoking memories of travel and holidays for some and dreams of distant lands for others. Children will want to pilot the aircraft or tend to the needs of passengers or act as holiday-makers travelling to exotic places. Although the airliner can be a starting point for developing all areas of the curriculum, the natural focus will be towards language, and scientific and geographical learning.

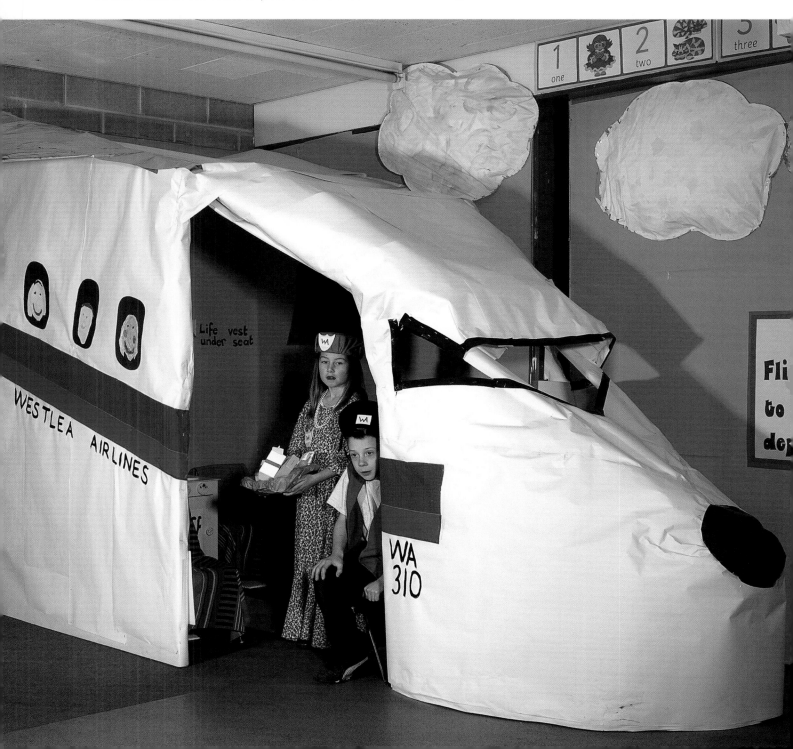

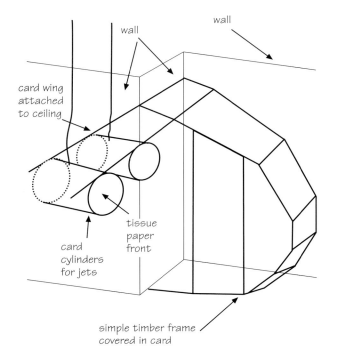

wall

wall

card wing attached to ceiling

card cylinders for jets

tissue paper front

simple timber frame covered in card

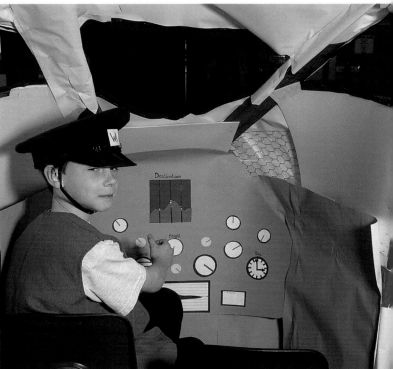

Setting up your play corner

The thought of constructing an airliner can be quite daunting, but for the brave and imaginative a simple frame covered in light cardboard is very effective (see diagram above). A cardboard wing can be suspended from the ceiling. Jet engines can be created with light-weight card cylinders and tissue paper. After installing colour co-ordinated seating for the passengers, with pockets for 'sick' bags, brochures etc, the interior can include windows with changeable views (fixed with Velcro). A variety of appropriate airline symbols and information signs can also be displayed.

No aircraft would be complete without a cockpit. A flight display panel can be created with a variety of attached dials, levers and switches. Small battery-driven bulbs can be included to add to its realism. As a final touch, an in-flight video screen can be made from a modified box and children can design their own favourite cartoons and screen images, which can be changed around using Velcro.

Specialised vocabulary

Aircraft words *e.g.* propeller, aisle, wing, cockpit, baggage hold, undercarriage
Flying words *e.g.* take-off, landing, turbulence
In-flight words *e.g.* duty-free, emergency procedures, sick bag, no smoking, in-flight entertainment
Airport words *e.g.* baggage claim, customs, announcement, passports, check-in, x-ray
Weather words *e.g.* cloudy, fog, visibility, sunset, storm, hail, clear skies
Food words *e.g.* menu, beverages, dessert, continental breakfast, sundae, cocktails, spirits
Cockpit dialogue *e.g.* pre-flight check, altitude, cruising speed, engine thrust, fuel level
Fun phrases *e.g.* fasten your seat belts, prepare for take-off and landing, this is a non-smoking flight, this is your captain speaking, the duty-free trolley will soon pass down the aisle

Jet airliner

Language development

- writing menus
- designing safety leaflets
- writing a diary describing what you see through the window of the plane
- recording a tape for in-flight instructions
- announcements and pilot information
- making badges for the crew
- designing the duty-free price list
- order form and sales sheet
- making a duty-free brochure
- writing instructions to go on signs and labels
- designing airline emblems and logos
- making passports and customs checks forms
- taping an in-flight entertainment programme
- designing a customer comment form
- making luggage labels and travel tickets
- creating a children's travel pack with games and items to occupy them during the flight
- reading newspapers, magazines and travel brochures on board
- making maps and charts of the flight path

Possible characters

There are numerous possibilities for creating exciting characters for airline passengers and the children will undoubtedly be highly inventive themselves. Here are some suggestions:

Crew and staff: pilot, flight attendants, customs control officer, flight mechanic, cleaner

Passengers: young, old, bossy, frightened of flying, airsick, foreign passengers, a celebrity, a rich person in first class, business travellers, holiday travellers, children travelling alone

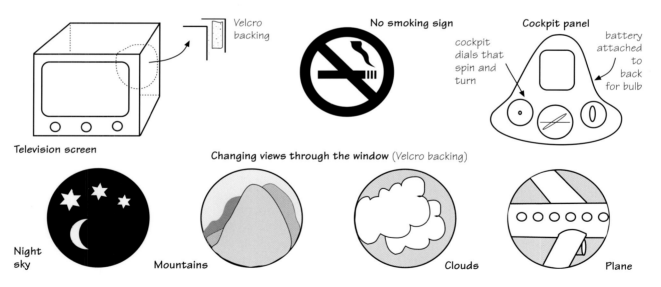

Television screen — Velcro backing

No smoking sign

Cockpit panel — cockpit dials that spin and turn — battery attached to back for bulb

Changing views through the window (Velcro backing)

Night sky

Mountains

Clouds

Plane

Props and accessories

Airlines and aircraft give scope for a wealth of artefacts and accessories. The class will enjoy choosing the airline's livery and designing and making the props.

These could include: emergency procedures pamphlets, menus, duty-free items and price lists, meal trays, food, children's travel fun bag, maps, passports, luggage labels, luggage, tickets, holiday clothes, in-flight magazines, sick bags, trolley, foreign currency, holiday brochures, magazines, newspapers, individual video screens, signs and labels, seats with seat-belts, headrests with covers, blankets, mechanic's tools, tape recorder for announcements, headphones for pilot.

Structured play opportunities

- take-off and landing
- a celebrity is on board
- crash landing
- in-flight entertainment
- a troubled flight
- dinner is served
- duty-free goods are available
- a flight to an exotic destination
- a crew member or a passenger falls ill
- training for the crew
- cooking for first class
- cleaning between meals/flights
- maintenance work
- pre-flight checks and tests
- your flight is delayed
- baggage check
- lost baggage
- customs control
- a visit to the cockpit
- caught with extra duty-free items!

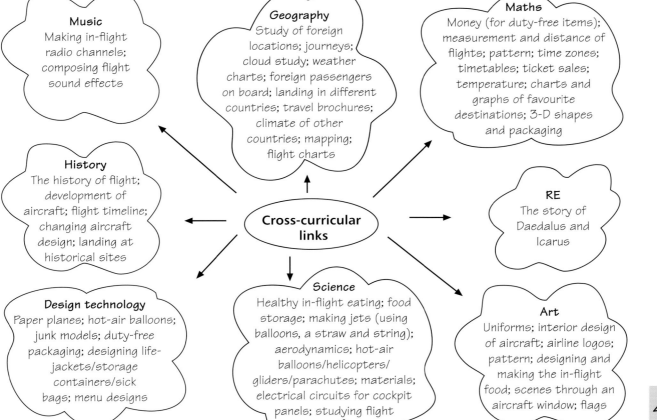

Music
Making in-flight radio channels; composing flight sound effects

Geography
Study of foreign locations; journeys; cloud study; weather charts; foreign passengers on board; landing in different countries; travel brochures; climate of other countries; mapping; flight charts

Maths
Money (for duty-free items); measurement and distance of flights; pattern; time zones; timetables; ticket sales; temperature; charts and graphs of favourite destinations; 3-D shapes and packaging

History
The history of flight; development of aircraft; flight timeline; changing aircraft design; landing at historical sites

Cross-curricular links

RE
The story of Daedalus and Icarus

Design technology
Paper planes; hot-air balloons; junk models; duty-free packaging; designing life-jackets/storage containers/sick bags; menu designs

Science
Healthy in-flight eating; food storage; making jets (using balloons, a straw and string); aerodynamics; hot-air balloons/helicopters/gliders/parachutes; materials; electrical circuits for cockpit panels; studying flight

Art
Uniforms; interior design of aircraft; airline logos; pattern; designing and making the in-flight food; scenes through an aircraft window; flags

Pirate ship

Introduction

Pirates have always intrigued children and imaginations can run riot at the very mention of Blackbeard or Long John Silver! A pirate ship will stimulate a great deal of historical research and will extend geographical skills and knowledge such as mapping, exploring physical aspects of landscapes and learning about foreign destinations.

Props and accessories

By its very nature, a pirate ship is always laden with secret cargo, everyday utensils, deadly weapons and precious treasures. The temptation is to make the ship so full that there is no room for the children to play! Different props can be introduced each week to avoid congestion. Barrels can be borrowed from friendly breweries and maps can be 'aged' by soaking in tea!

Suggestions for props are: ship's wheel, cannon, quill, maps, tankards, treasure chest, telescopes, flags, anchor, compass, parrot, bottles, supplies, jewellery, buckets and brushes, swords, cannon balls, hammock, log book, food, treasure, lanterns.

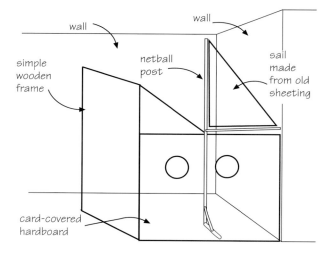

Construction hints

Use old sheeting for the sail. The main body of the boat can be created with card. Discarded cardboard containers from electrical equipment showrooms are ideal. Rigging can be created from school skipping ropes or string. The main mast needs to be sturdy - a netball post and stand can be adapted or use a wooden pole secured in a garden umbrella base.

Structured play opportunities

- setting sail
- discovering treasure
- spring cleaning
- picking up a message in a bottle
- cooking a pirate dinner
- sharing the treasure
- sailor overboard
- a ghost ship
- stowaway
- adrift with stocks running low
- scuttling a Spanish treasure ship
- a night ashore
- swallowed by a whale
- evening entertainment
- searching for land
- the trial and walking the plank
- robbing a ship
- sinking in a storm
- a pirate party
- mutiny
- the shipwreck
- attack by sharks
- nightfall and sea shanties
- undersea adventure

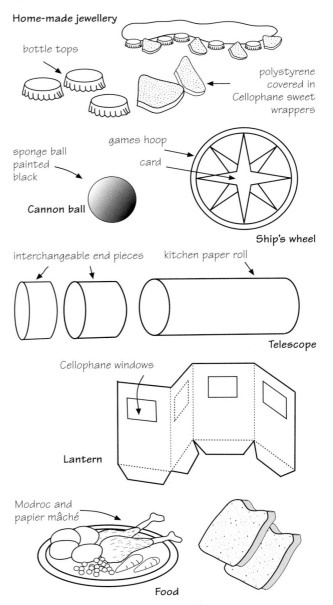

Possible characters

Pirates: Captain Hook, Blackbeard, Long John Silver, pirates galore, enemy pirates
Crew: captain, navigator, cook, lookout, doctor, boatswain
Shipmates: sail-menders/makers, knotter, carpenter, ship builder, storeman/woman
Others: captive sailors, castaway, deserter, mutineer, stowaway, mermaids/mermen, natives, cannibals, scientists, explorers

Home-made jewellery

bottle tops

polystyrene covered in Cellophane sweet wrappers

sponge ball painted black

games hoop

card

Cannon ball

Ship's wheel

interchangeable end pieces

kitchen paper roll

Telescope

Cellophane windows

Lantern

Modroc and papier mâché

Food

Pirate ship

Specialised vocabulary

Weather terms *e.g. storm, rainbow, tornado*
Nautical terms *e.g. starboard, port, stern*
Ship features *e.g. rigging, porthole, deck, hatch*
Weapons *e.g. cutlass, cannon, ramrod*
Sealife vocabulary *e.g. seaweed, coral, seabed*
Landscape vocabulary *e.g. horizon, island, iceberg*
Exploration terms *e.g. voyage, discovery, expedition*
Harbour words *e.g. cargo, provisions*
Fun phrases *e.g. mutiny aboard, me hearties, pieces-of-eight, land ahoy! Ho, ho, ho and a bottle of rum!*

Backdrop ideas

Sky, weather conditions, icebergs, horizons, a spouting whale, volcanoes, a sea-battle scene, distant islands, stormy seas, a Spanish galleon, the harbourside.

Language development

- writing letters home to the family
- drawing and using maps
- writing a pirate dinner menu
- writing messages to put in a bottle
- pirate job rotas
- pirate supplies
- shopping lists
- pirate recruitment posters
- instructions for doing jobs (e.g. loading a cannon)
- safety rules on board ship
- pirate log book and diary
- 'wanted' posters
- a pirate song

Space rocket

Introduction

Most children dream of travelling to the moon. Their imagination is captured by the idea of space rockets, aliens and space travel. Children will be eager to take their first steps on to the lunar landscape, fire laser guns at invading Martians or move weightlessly around the spacecraft. As few children will have visited Cape Kennedy in the USA and seen a real rocket, the inclusion of a play rocket in the classroom will provide a rare opportunity for them to investigate the wonders of science. The children's play will undoubtedly 'lift-off'!

Construction hints

The adventurous builder can construct elaborate rockets with fuel tanks, detachable nose pieces and booster engines. However, a simple cylindrical or rectangular frame covered with card or foil is sufficient. When painted and with wings and nose added, the rocket will look almost real enough to take-off (see photograph on page 49).

The lunar surface can be re-created by covering the floor with black material and adding craters and boulders made from chicken-wire moulds and papier mâché. Special effects - such as real flashing lights and a tape recording of countdown, blast off and the link up with mission control coming from a concealed recorder in the rocket - will add a new dimension to the children's play.

An alternative to a rocket is a time machine similar to Dr Who's 'Tardis'. This gives opportunities for both space travel and travel through time into the future and back to the past (see photograph above and diagram on the right).

Possible characters

Staff: astronauts, mission control personnel, engineers, scientists, supplies loaders, mechanics, cleaners, radar operators
Others: aliens, family and friends, the Prime Minister, the Queen, stowaways, a thief, characters from TV and films such as Dr Who or Mr Spock

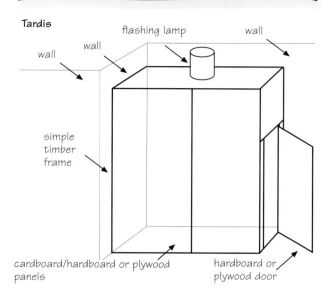

Tardis — flashing lamp — wall — wall — wall — simple timber frame — cardboard/hardboard or plywood panels — hardboard or plywood door

Space rocket

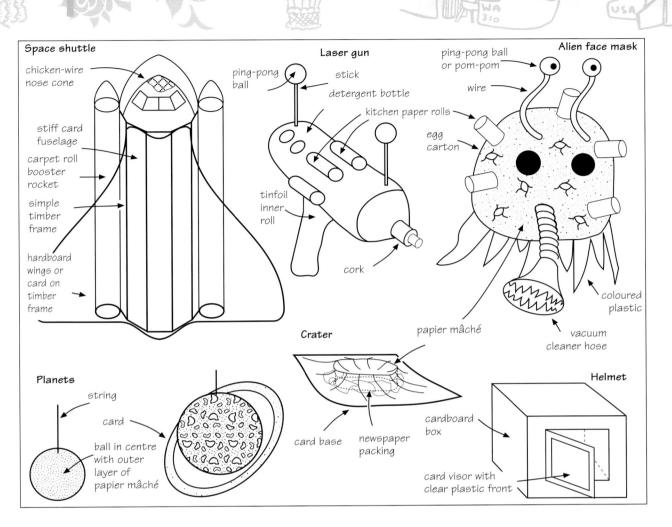

Space shuttle
- chicken-wire nose cone
- stiff card fuselage
- carpet roll booster rocket
- simple timber frame
- hardboard wings or card on timber frame

Laser gun
- ping-pong ball
- stick
- detergent bottle
- kitchen paper rolls
- tinfoil inner roll
- cork

Alien face mask
- ping-pong ball or pom-pom
- wire
- egg carton
- papier mâché
- vacuum cleaner hose
- coloured plastic

Planets
- string
- card
- ball in centre with outer layer of papier mâché

Crater
- card base
- newspaper packing

Helmet
- cardboard box
- card visor with clear plastic front

Props and accessories

Planets on strings suspended from the ceiling, radar, laser guns, tool kit, spare food, cleaning materials, go-kart moon buggy, moon boots, backpacks, fuel tanks, telescope, fire blanket, radio, headphones, camera, flag, first aid kit, sick bags, maps, charts of stars, computer.

Language development

• log books • letters home • diaries • weather reports • taped conversations with mission control • job description for an astronaut • repair manuals • the planets - fact books • astronomical charts • instructions on how to use equipment • safety procedures • writing in Martian language • coded messages

Structured play opportunities

- the launch
- lost in space
- meals in space
- living in space
- landing on the moon or another planet
- alien attack
- speaking to mission control
- moon walk
- repairs to the rocket
- a meteor is sighted
- breakdown and power failure
- illness on board
- a fire
- preparing for lift-off
- preparing to land
- communicating by satellite with families
- a birthday aboard
- loading supplies

Canal barge

Introduction

An excellent way of combining cross-curricular studies in history, geography, art, science and technology is by creating a canal barge in the learning corner. Life on barges is steeped in traditions and customs, providing interesting starting points for play in both the present and the past. Children can dress in modern or traditional clothing and their play will centre upon domestic life on board the barge or pretend travel along the canal bank.

Setting up your play corner

As space in a classroom is often at a premium, there is no need to build a full-length boat. A barge emerging from a tunnel can look highly effective and will stimulate exciting indoor and outdoor play.

Once the main structure of the barge has been completed, a decision needs to be made about the boat's character. Will it have a modern or traditional interior? Home corner furniture can be used inside and the children will enjoy decorating the outside with authentic canal art designs. It is important to paint the backdrop before construction work begins.

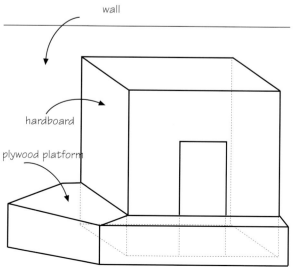

wall

hardboard

plywood platform

Props and accessories

Canal art is now very popular and designs are bright, bold and simple for children to replicate. Almost any household utensil such as a bucket, plate, wooden spoon or mug can be decorated fairly cheaply to look authentic. Local canal art experts will often visit schools and several well-illustrated books are available. Craft fairs can also be productive hunting grounds for inexpensive artefacts.

Possible props that could be included on board are: tool kit, washing line, cooking utensils, rope, buoys, pretend food, fishing rods and nets, board games to play on the barge, cutlery, buckets, lanterns, life-jackets, baskets, radio, maps, paint pots and brushes, crockery, pots and pans, picnic basket, anchor, cleaning materials, plumb line, rag mats.

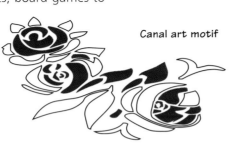

Backdrop ideas

Canal bank, lock-keeper's house, landscapes, an inn, industrial buildings, a tunnel wall, cottages, woodland, inside a lock, other passing boats, the wharfside, a shop, a farm.

Decorated lantern

Canal art motif

Structured play opportunities

- spring cleaning the barge
- setting off on holiday
- cooking supper
- meeting up with fellow barge people
- washing, mending and drying clothes
- travelling through a lock
- buying supplies
- friends arriving
- fire on board
- selling crafts
- relatives arrive
- the injury
- the breakdown
- singing canal songs and playing games
- repairing and decorating
- a party on board
- a night by the canal
- schooling on board
- a picnic
- springing a leak
- the crash!

- boat/barge for sale
- loading provisions
- tourists on board
- mice on board
- a family illness - the doctor is called

Canal barge

Language development

- writing to relatives and friends
- a canal barge diary
- selling the boat - sales details for prospective buyers
- canal songs
- making a tape of canal bank noises - voices and sounds
- shopping list
- price list for crafts on sale
- advertising a barge holiday
- school work
- party invitations
- recipes

Specialised vocabulary

Boat words e.g. rudder, deck, bow, anchor, berth
Canal words e.g. bank, lock, tow-path
Landscape words e.g. valley, hills, wood, copse
Mechanical words e.g. crankshaft, tank, piston
Professions e.g. doctor, lock-keeper, captain
Tools e.g. spanner, screwdriver, hammer, wrench
Utensils e.g. mug, basket, tray, ladle
Furniture e.g. table, bunks, cooker
Water words e.g. depth, wave, wake, ripples, oxbow
Food/meal words e.g. lunch, supper, dinner, picnic
Structural words e.g. tunnel, bridge, lock, weir
Plants/wildlife e.g. duck, swan, rushes, iris, pike

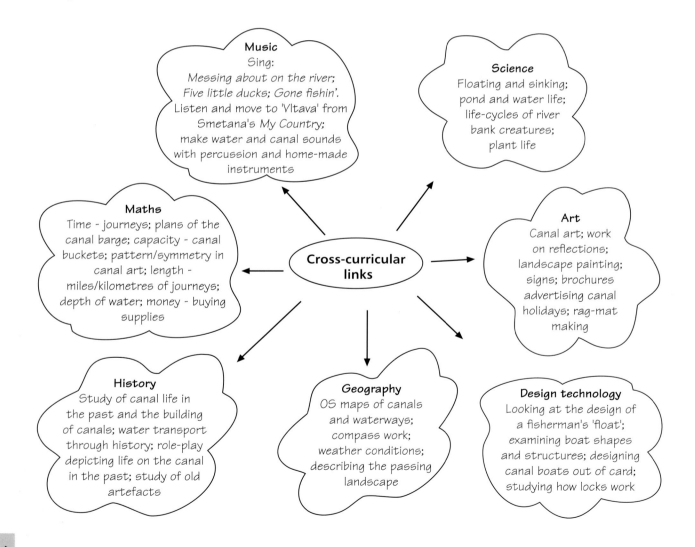

Music
Sing:
*Messing about on the river;
Five little ducks; Gone fishin'.*
Listen and move to 'Vltava' from Smetana's *My Country;*
make water and canal sounds with percussion and home-made instruments

Science
Floating and sinking; pond and water life; life-cycles of river bank creatures; plant life

Maths
Time - journeys; plans of the canal barge; capacity - canal buckets; pattern/symmetry in canal art; length - miles/kilometres of journeys; depth of water; money - buying supplies

Cross-curricular links

Art
Canal art; work on reflections; landscape painting; signs; brochures advertising canal holidays; rag-mat making

History
Study of canal life in the past and the building of canals; water transport through history; role-play depicting life on the canal in the past; study of old artefacts

Geography
OS maps of canals and waterways; compass work; weather conditions; describing the passing landscape

Design technology
Looking at the design of a fisherman's 'float'; examining boat shapes and structures; designing canal boats out of card; studying how locks work

Hot-air balloon

Introduction

A hot-air balloon floating effortlessly through the sky makes people stop and stare. Its silence and bright colours create a magical atmosphere. Imagine what a wonderful surprise it is for children when a hot-air balloon actually 'lands' in their classroom for them to play in. Soon the children will be loading supplies and clambering aboard to float off to destinations far, far away.

Construction hints

The balloon basket is a simple, square wooden structure covered in card or brown paper. The card is sponged to give a basket effect. A doorway is cut out and a balloon canopy is created above with either fabric or a parachute. (Parachutes can sometimes be obtained from flying clubs or air force bases.) Strings are then attached to the basket.

Props and accessories

Weights, sandbags, picnic basket, maps, telescope, repair kit, blanket, camera, first aid kit, fire extinguisher, rations, supplies, rope, clothing.

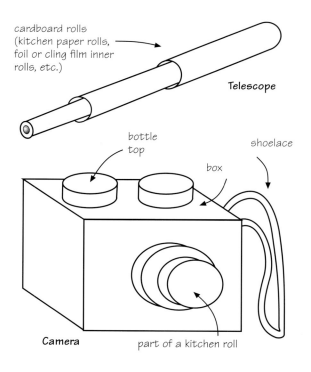

cardboard rolls (kitchen paper rolls, foil or cling film inner rolls, etc.)

Telescope

bottle top

shoelace

box

Camera

part of a kitchen roll

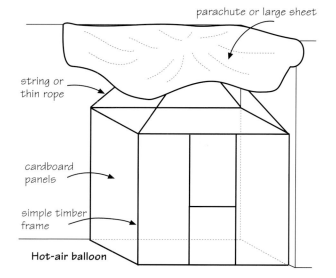

parachute or large sheet

string or thin rope

cardboard panels

simple timber frame

Hot-air balloon

Hot-air balloon

Landing destinations

Jungle, farm, sea, the North Pole, mountain tops, swamp, river, forest, desert, beach, park, island, town, city.

Language development

• posters about flight • maps • leaflets • charts • weather reports • instructions for inflating a hot-air balloon

Possible characters

Pilot, ground crew, balloon maker, family members, passengers, celebrity guests, ambulance crew, firefighters, residents of foreign lands, safety experts

Structured play opportunities

• a flight around the world in 80 days
• crash landing
• loading supplies
• landing and lost on a desert island
• landing in different parts of the world, e.g Africa, the North Pole
• hot-air balloon race
• night flight
• fire on board
• storm
• the escape
• spring clean
• mending day
• take-off at a summer fête
• hot-air balloon festival

57

Tudor house and ship

Introduction

Bringing history to life is essential for young children. Schools are not always fortunate enough to be situated near to historical sites, so children's experiences are often second-hand through reference materials, slides or TV programmes.

Historical provision can be greatly enhanced by the creation of learning corners where children can handle authentic artefacts, act out historical drama, take on the role of famous characters in history and imagine what life was like long, long ago.

There are plenty of historical eras or themes to choose from that will appeal to young children's curiosity. A stone-age cave, a Roman villa, a Victorian kitchen or an iron-age hut could transform a corner of the classroom.

In the photographs below, two adjoining classes chose to build a Tudor house and ship to stimulate learning through role-play. Weeks of research ensured that both constructions were accurate replicas. Visitors to these classrooms were regularly treated to performances by the children of 'Elizabethan drama' at its best!

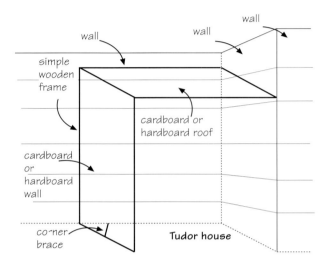

wall
wall
wall
simple wooden frame
cardboard or hardboard roof
cardboard or hardboard wall
corner brace

Tudor house

Construction hints

The Mary Rose ship

The house is a simple wooden frame with an interior full of artefacts, some of which were made by the children. The other items were borrowed from a local museum service. The ship is constructed on a simple timber frame. The upright timbers slope inwards at the base to create the effect of a ship's hull. Horizontal timbers are fixed at the base, middle and top of the frame to form a rigid structure.

Slots for the cannons are made from pairs of battens fixed to the horizontal timbers. Each pair holds its cannon in place by squeezing it slightly.

The cladding is made from long strips of cardboard wrapped in creased paper. Beginning at the base, each strip is fixed to the frame - just overlapping the strip below it.

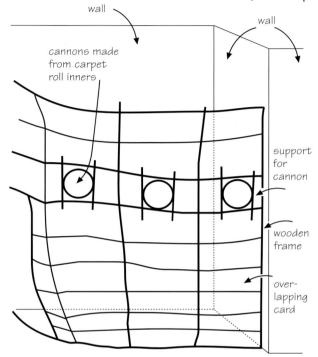

Props and accessories

Compasses, table covered with cloth, stool, basket of clothes, lantern, wooden bowls/plates/spoons, pewter tankards/plates/spoons, old working tools (made safe), bowl of apples, 'parchment' pieces, sundials, shelving for artefacts, wooden boxes, rigging (skipping rope), cannon balls, chests/boxes, candlesticks, reproduction coinage, quill pens and ink, brown glazed bowls, framed portraits of Tudor royalty, Tudor games and toys, fire basket and fireback, reproduction pottery including Tudor Greenware, small bottles for herbal remedies, mortar and pestle, torn sail to repair.

Portrait of Tudor monarch in frame

frame is wrapped in papier mâché and painted gold

Tudor house and ship

Craft activities

1. Make a pomander using an orange and cloves. Tie a ribbon around it.

Pomander

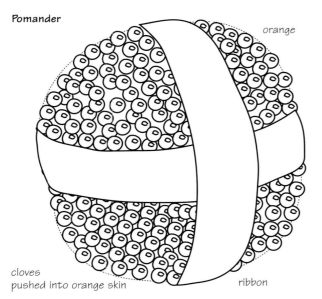

cloves
pushed into orange skin

orange

ribbon

Clay Tudor rose

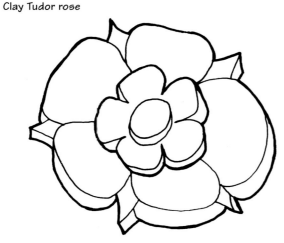

2. Make a clay Tudor rose.

3. Make a bookmark using a quill to write on it. Decorate it with Tudor roses or Tudor-style patterns.

4. Design a knot garden. Use cross-stitch to sew your design.

5. Design and print your own seal.

6. Make a clay plaque of a Tudor house.

Clay Tudor house plaque

7. Use Fimo to make reproduction jewellery (check famous Tudor portraits for reference). Make a jewel casket for Elizabeth I.

Language development

• a shopping list for a grand banquet • a letter describing preparations for a visit by the Queen • a survivor's diary account of the sinking of the *Mary Rose* ship • an inventory of equipment to take on a voyage • inventory of the house • newspaper report of the defeat of the Spanish Armada • poster to recruit sailors • instructions for loading a cannon or making Tudor food • 'hot seating' a Spanish/English sailor, a servant/owner • use coins, quills and ink to produce household accounts • write and perform a play to entertain a visitor

Possible characters

House: the Master, the Mistress, their children, the music/dancing teacher, a messenger from the Queen, an apothecary/physician, the tutor, pedlars, a soldier
Ship: captain, sailors, ship's surgeon, pilot, archer, gunner, watchman/woman, carpenter, barber, cook

Structured play opportunities

• make simple Tudor remedies - honey and garlic for a sore throat and apple and frankincense for a 'pain in the side'
• set the table for the servants' meal
• set the table for a meal for the Master
• play with a Tudor toy or game
• use the clothes to portray a character
• preparing and serving a meal
• sighting land after a long voyage
• set up the cabin of the surgeon, captain or carpenter
• sighting the Spanish Armada - action stations!
• boarded by pirates
• Tudor games and pastimes

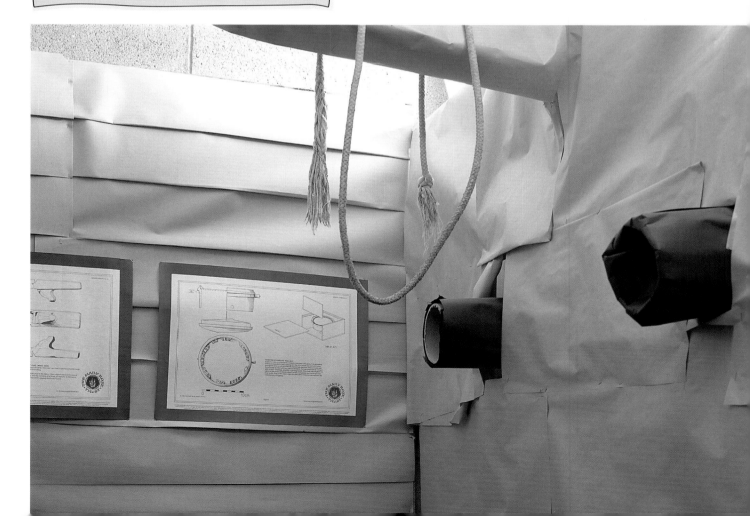

Introduction

Children who have not visited a real castle will probably have seen some lively images from films and fairy tales. Unfortunately, these 'snapshots' are often misleading and give the impression that all castles were constantly besieged by marauding knights and fierce dragons, or were always home to kings, queens and distressed damsels! The existence of a classroom castle will bring history to life and give children the opportunity to explore and experience aspects of everyday living in past times.

Construction hints

If a corner of the classroom is used, only two sides of the castle will need to be constructed. These can be made from stiff card, but light-weight hardboard will produce a sturdier structure. Small slits will serve as windows. These can be painted on or cut out.

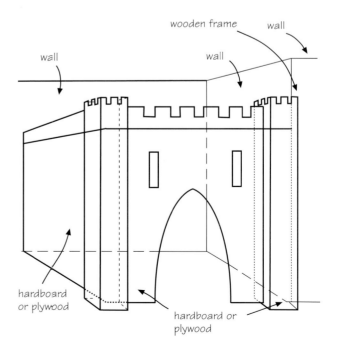

wooden frame

wall

wall

wall

hardboard or plywood

hardboard or plywood

Castle

There are two styles of gate protection to choose from - a drawbridge or a portcullis. A working model of either one of these will enhance play provision and thrill the children (see diagrams below). The castle's interior will need an open fireplace and other suitable traditional furniture, and sheepskin rugs give an authentic feel underfoot.

Possible characters

Kings, queens, princesses, princes, maidens, knights, visiting aristocracy, carpenter, friars, jugglers, magicians, jesters, cooks, blacksmith, storeman/woman, bishops, acrobats, a sorcerer, minstrels, chambermaids, servants, cleaners, armour maker, peasants, barons, dancers

Props and accessories

Parents will often help to make wooden swords and shields. Flags can be produced from old sheeting painted with a mixture of PVA glue and paint. Simple knights' helmets and damsels' bonnets can be made from card. Papier mâché food such as chicken legs, a boar's head and other traditional banquet food can look highly effective, and plastic bowls can be covered in foil to give a pewter effect.

Props could include: quill pens, sheepskin rugs, bows and arrows, pots and pans, goblets, crowns, cleaning materials, kitchen utensils, swords, tapestries, juggling balls, jewellery, tools, lanterns, banners, ball and chain, cutlery, musical instruments, treasure.

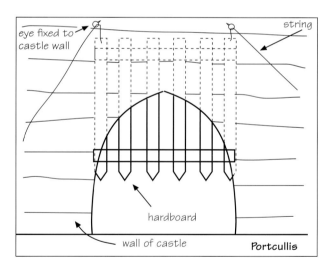

eye fixed to castle wall

string

hardboard

wall of castle

Portcullis

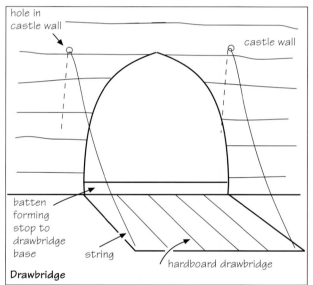

hole in castle wall

castle wall

batten forming stop to drawbridge base

string

hardboard drawbridge

Drawbridge

Food

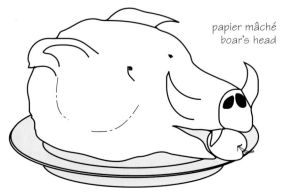

papier mâché boar's head

papier mâché chicken drumsticks and potatoes

tinfoil over paper plate to give pewter effect

63

Structured play opportunities

If the children are offered rich structured play opportunities, their ideas will quickly change as they realise that the knight's shining armour actually had to be cleaned regularly. Children will also discover that extravagant banquets meant hours of preparation in a stiflingly hot kitchen deep beneath the castle's staterooms. However, a castle should also be the source of imaginative play, where fact becomes fantasy and princesses are rescued by princes who have fought off fire-breathing dragons to reach them.

Play opportunities could include:
• preparing for a banquet
• the feast
• preparing for a jousting tournament - designing banners and shields
• the minstrels and jesters entertain
• acting out fairy tales such as *Sleeping Beauty* or *Jack and the Beanstalk*
• the coronation

Language development

• producing an historical guide or leaflet about the castle
• making up a family tree
• banquet menus
• diary of a knight
• maps and plans of the castle
• writing and performing a guided tour
• instructions for cleaning armour, etc
• writing letters with a wax seal
• making an inventory of weapons
• food order for the kitchen
• party, wedding and coronation invitations
• reception table plan with names
• battle orders and battle plan
• preparing for a siege
• spring cleaning
• the royal wedding
• a guided tour of the castle
• haunted rooms!

Specialised vocabulary

Clothing *e.g.* armour, chain-mail, visor, ruff
Personnel *e.g.* jester, blacksmith, cook, minstrel
Castle words *e.g.* moat, drawbridge, portcullis, ramparts
Battle words *e.g.* siege, battalion, charge!
Weapons *e.g.* sword, shield, rapier, longbow, crossbow
Furniture *e.g.* throne, spit, four-poster bed

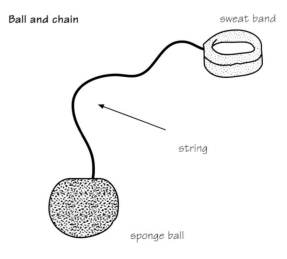

Ball and chain

sweat band

string

sponge ball

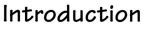

Introduction

Many children make regular visits to museums with their parents and with their schools. Primary school teachers make excellent use of museum and library services to borrow artefacts to enrich historical studies. Both these aspects can be successfully brought together in a classroom museum, which will give a real context for historical research and stimulate interest in objects from the past. A museum learning corner has a wide appeal, as different classes in the school can make use of it to further their skills, widen their knowledge and increase their understanding of antique objects.

Construction hints

Little exterior work is needed when creating a museum - a simple sign is adequate. A walk-in cupboard, store room or quiet room can be used.

However, space for displaying and handling objects is essential. Simple shelving can be erected, and tables or boxes covered in material will make good viewing areas. Labels and information cards are very important, and temporary spot lighting creates an authentic atmosphere and feel to the museum.

Props and accessories

The contents of the museum will rely upon objects acquired from home and from loans services, and those available in the school's own resource collections. The range of artefacts on display could follow a theme such as 'Victorian exhibition' or 'Portraits from the 1800s'. Enormous fun can be had when children make their own museum exhibits, using a variety of design and ageing techniques to produce convincing replicas. Here are a few examples:

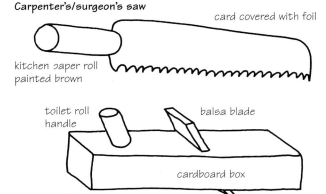

Carpenter's/surgeon's saw

card covered with foil

kitchen paper roll painted brown

toilet roll handle

balsa blade

cardboard box

Carpenter's plane

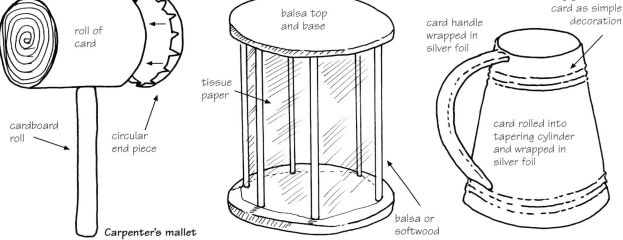

roll of card

circular end piece

cardboard roll

Carpenter's mallet

Lantern

balsa top and base

tissue paper

balsa or softwood

Pewter tankard

string glued onto card as simple decoration

card handle wrapped in silver foil

card rolled into tapering cylinder and wrapped in silver foil

Structured play opportunities

- the first day
- theft of a precious artefact
- new arrivals
- spring clean
- guided tours
- stock-taking
- valuations
- the Antiques Roadshow visits
- a new exhibition is prepared
- the Queen visits
- a school party arrives
- a precious object is accidentally broken
- Expert Day - experts are available to discuss items with the general public
- Open Day
- the museum is threatened with closure

Specialised vocabulary

Historical eras *e.g.* Victorian, Georgian, Elizabethan
Historical vocabulary *e.g.* ancient, old, antique, past
Artefacts *e.g.* mangle, musket, fossil, goblet
Descriptive words *e.g.* precious, priceless, damaged, authentic, replica
Artefact parts *e.g.* handle, spokes, trigger, buckle

Language development

• catalogues • adverts • posters • descriptions and information about artefacts • users' guide • pamphlets • guided tours on an audio tape to hear through headphones as you walk around the museum • museum floor plans • stock-take and audit • instructions for staff • staff work rotas • writing guided tours (children can read these out for visitors) • research articles • valuations (written and over the phone)

Nursery rhyme cottage

Introduction

The importance of a child regularly experiencing nursery rhymes and fairy tales in the early and formative stages of his or her language development cannot be emphasised enough. Nursery rhymes and fairy tales are a source of rich language and provide experience of rhyme and rhythm. The nursery rhyme and fairy tale cottage offers class teachers numerous starting points to stimulate and extend language and imagination as the children become absorbed in their play.

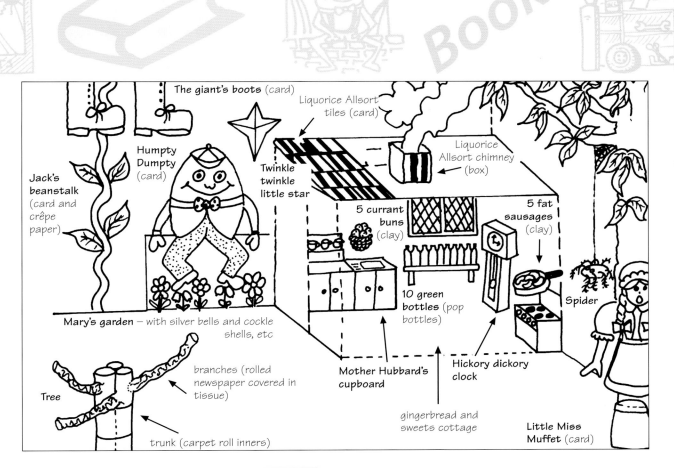

The giant's boots (card)

Liquorice Allsort tiles (card)

Humpty Dumpty (card)

Liquorice Allsort chimney (box)

Twinkle twinkle little star

Jack's beanstalk (card and crêpe paper)

5 currant buns (clay)

5 fat sausages (clay)

10 green bottles (pop bottles)

Spider

Mary's garden – with silver bells and cockle shells, etc

Mother Hubbard's cupboard

Hickory dickory clock

branches (rolled newspaper covered in tissue)

Tree

gingerbread and sweets cottage

Little Miss Muffet (card)

trunk (carpet roll inners)

Setting up your play corner

Once the basic cottage structure has been built, it can be brightly decorated with 'sweets' artwork. A painted box easily converts into a Liquorice Allsort chimney (cotton wool smoke will add to the authenticity), which can sit on Allsorts roof tiles.

Then begins the exciting task of deciding which nursery rhyme and fairy tale characters to include in your play corner. The children will already know many rhymes and stories and together you can customise the corner according to favourite choices. Externally there is the potential for gardens and forest, while internally the cottage will offer opportunities for rhymes such as *Three blind mice, Hickory dickory dock,* and *Polly, put the kettle on.*

Additional nursery rhymes that could be included in the corner are: *Incey wincey spider, Old King Cole, The queen of hearts, Ladybird, ladybird,* and *This is the way we wash our clothes.*

Props and accessories

Miss Muffet's spider

(pom-pom and pipe cleaners)

Miss Muffet's tuffet

(bucket covered in green tissue and sponge printed)

Liquorice Allsort chimney

(cardboard box – painted)

Possible sweets decorations

Liquorice Allsorts (coloured paper and black paint)

Jellybeans (white paint to give 3-D effect)

Gingerbread figures (sugar paper)

Hickory dickory clock

(boxes joined together and covered in brown paper with pattern painted on, plastic clock nailed on)

Candy sticks (red paper and white paint)

Smarties (coloured paper and white paint)

Toffees (Cellophane or crêpe paper)

Additional props

Humpty Dumpty	10 green bottles	Twinkle star
Little Miss Muffet	5 fat sausages	Flowers, shells, silver bells
Baa Baa Black Sheep	5 currant buns	Hey diddle diddle mobile
	Polly's kettle	

Structured play opportunities

• caring for Mary's garden • letter from the giant - prepare a giant-sized meal and clean the house • Little Miss Muffet's birthday party - send out invitations and prepare the party • the King's men are coming to try to mend Humpty Dumpty but they have got lost - can you help them find their way using a map? • Old Mother Hubbard's cupboard is bare - make a shopping list and go to the class shop to buy some food • Little Miss Muffet is fed up with eating curds and whey - make her some new meals (use play dough) • Baa Baa Black Sheep's wool needs to be sorted into three bags and then delivered • act out nursery rhymes • look after nursery rhyme characters • make up pretend rhymes • 'Who am I?' - pretend to be a character for others to guess • having characters to stay overnight • washday for characters • hunt the nursery rhyme • nursery rhyme theme party • visitors for the day

Language development

• nursery rhymes on tape • singing and telling nursery rhymes • rhyming words on labels • sending letters • party invitations • drawing the story of a nursery rhyme • shopping lists • phone messages • nursery rhyme books • sequencing nursery rhymes • changing endings to rhymes • writing menus

Specialised vocabulary

Animals e.g. dog, cat, sheep
Characters e.g. Humpty Dumpty, Little Miss Muffet, the giant
Names e.g. Jack, Mary, Polly
Places e.g. the giant's castle, Hansel and Gretel's cottage, Little Miss Muffet's tuffet
Objects e.g. kettle, clock, wall
Counting e.g. counting rhymes, numbers, ordering
'Doing' words e.g. cooking, running, jumping

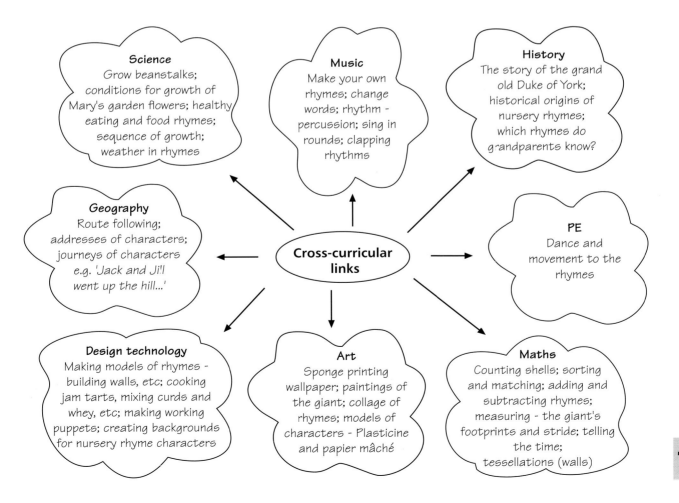

Science
Grow beanstalks; conditions for growth of Mary's garden flowers; healthy eating and food rhymes; sequence of growth; weather in rhymes

Music
Make your own rhymes; change words; rhythm - percussion; sing in rounds; clapping rhythms

History
The story of the grand old Duke of York; historical origins of nursery rhymes; which rhymes do grandparents know?

Geography
Route following; addresses of characters; journeys of characters e.g. 'Jack and Jill went up the hill...'

Cross-curricular links

PE
Dance and movement to the rhymes

Design technology
Making models of rhymes - building walls, etc; cooking jam tarts, mixing curds and whey, etc; making working puppets; creating backgrounds for nursery rhyme characters

Art
Sponge printing wallpaper; paintings of the giant; collage of rhymes; models of characters - Plasticine and papier mâché

Maths
Counting shells; sorting and matching; adding and subtracting rhymes; measuring - the giant's footprints and stride; telling the time; tessellations (walls)

Percy's hut

Introduction

Popular picture books can offer an appealing theme for play. There are plenty of stories to choose from and favourite characters such as Percy the park keeper from the book by Nick Butterworth will be high on the list. There is scope for re-creating the homes of characters, for outdoor and indoor story settings, and for individual scenes. The challenge for the teacher is to create a play corner that represents the story as closely as possible, since children will spot every difference from the original!

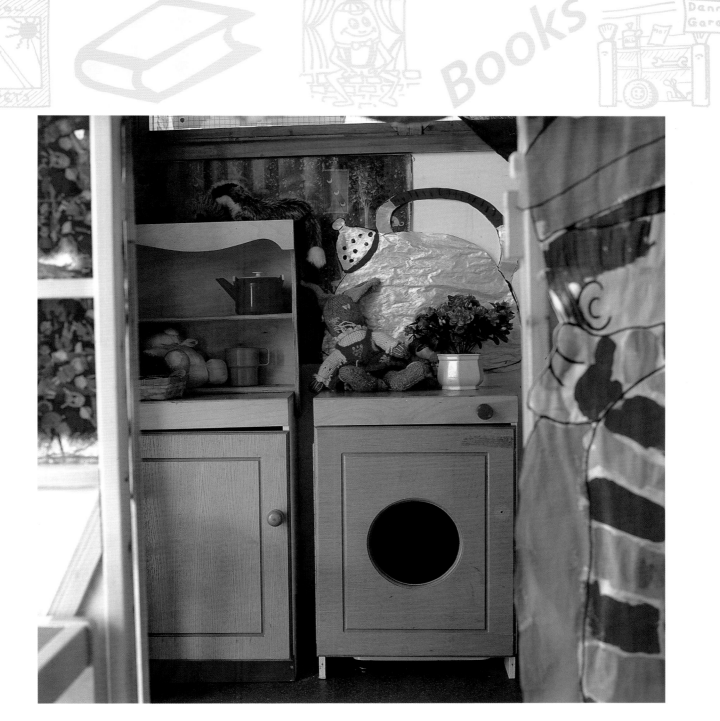

Structured play opportunities

The story will direct the structure of most of the play activities but here are some alternative suggestions:
• write new stories
• invent new characters
• change the personality of a character, e.g. Percy is grumpy and dislikes animals or Percy is careless and drops litter
• use the story setting for play that isn't associated with the true storyline, e.g. a picnic in Percy's hut or hiding from robbers in Percy's hut

Possible themes

The list of excellent picture books for play corners is enormous. Here are some to stimulate ideas: *Can't You Sleep, Little Bear?* (a cave); *Whatever Next?* (a rocket); *The Lighthouse Keeper's Lunch* (a lighthouse); *The Queen's Knickers* (a palace); *Funnybones* (a park); *Elmer* (a jungle); *Ruby* (a toy factory); *Pingu* (an igloo). See page 79 for additional suggestions.

Danny's garage

Introduction

A play corner that re-creates a scene from a fiction book can really bring a story to life for young children. It can help extend a child's understanding of plot, characters and setting, while providing a real context for creative role-play through which a storyline can be re-enacted again and again. Here the garage from *Danny the Champion of the World* by Roald Dahl also provides a useful base for a class's design technology work.

Setting up your play corner

The structure for the garage is a simple wooden frame with hardboard roof and sides. When re-creating a set from a story, accuracy is very important. The text must be scrutinised carefully to make sure that the final product closely replicates the one described in the story. This is a highly useful exercise in itself for testing children's comprehension and extending their observational skills.

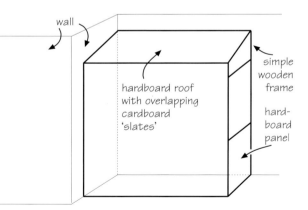

wall

hardboard roof with overlapping cardboard 'slates'

simple wooden frame

hard-board panel

Specialised vocabulary

Mechanical vocabulary e.g. engine, piston, spoke
Tools e.g. hacksaw, wrench, spanner, vice
Garage words e.g. pump, workshop, nozzle, pit
Vehicle words e.g. exhaust, steering wheel, hub cap
Repairs vocabulary e.g. weld, seal, tighten, bore, drill

Language development

A scene from a book will naturally have a strong language focus. Here are a few activities that can be adapted for any chosen story:

- re-enact the story
- create a new storyline while retaining the same setting
- write a play based on the original text to act in the play corner

- explore characters
- read the story aloud and act it out simultaneously
- explore and extend conversations that may or may not be included in the original text
- introduce new characters
- create completely new stories to act
- write a letter to a character in the book
- write a letter from a character in the book
- mime a scene from the book
- act out new scenes that take place after the book's original ending

Introduction

Look at the faces of children watching a puppet performance or a Punch and Judy show and you will see that they are completely absorbed in the make-believe world that has been created.

Puppets seem to hold an almost magnetic attraction for children. As a result, puppets are an excellent medium for encouraging storytelling and developing a child's language and conversational skills. A child's inhibitions and self-consciousness seem to disappear once a puppet is slipped over his or her hand. Children who are often timid and quiet find that they gain an inner confidence and can express themselves through their chosen character.

A puppet theatre is a good alternative to a play corner and is an ideal choice when space is limited.

Construction hints

It is not necessary to build a solid theatre as puppets can perform behind a simple partition or even on a child's knee. However, a theatre is not difficult to make (see page 77) and if it is made sufficiently light-weight and portable, it can be moved from one classroom to another. Enough space needs to be provided for three or four children to perform and a simple curtain will give a more professional touch to the show. For shadow puppet theatres, the performing area needs to be covered with a tracing paper or greaseproof paper frame and a lamp has to be fixed behind the performers.

Puppet theatre

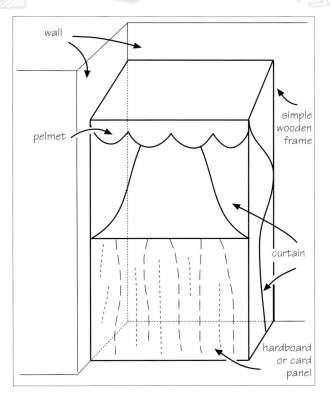

wall

pelmet

simple wooden frame

curtain

hardboard or card panel

wall

curtain

curtain

lower curtain for string puppet performance

Puppet theatre activities

• act out well-known stories and fairy tales • write and perform new plays and simple stories • mime and dance to music and songs • perform a musical show • perform a Punch and Judy show • use shadow puppets to act out traditional tales from around the world • tell jokes • pretend to be a ventriloquist • use puppets to give important information on topics of interest • act out a TV show with puppets • act out family roles • use puppets to develop free conversation in class

Types of puppet

• finger puppets • glove puppets • string puppets • shadow puppets • hand puppets • soft toys • junk puppets

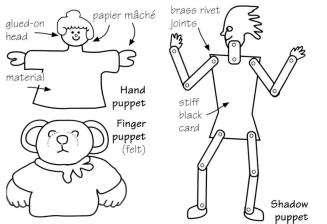

glued-on head

papier mâché

material

Hand puppet

Finger puppet (felt)

brass rivet joints

stiff black card

Shadow puppet

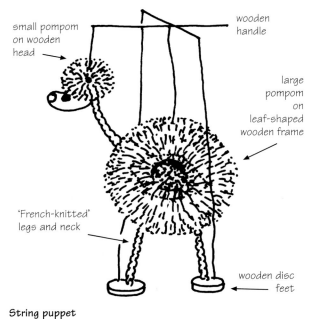

small pompom on wooden head

wooden handle

large pompom on leaf-shaped wooden frame

'French-knitted' legs and neck

wooden disc feet

String puppet

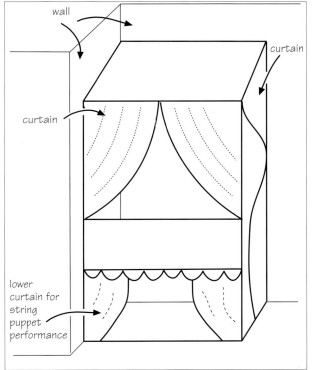

Hints and further ideas

Construction advice

Choose appropriate materials to make the construction of your play corners easy:

• The timber for the framework should be planed rather than sawn as the latter can produce splinters. Always use untreated timber to avoid contact with any possibly toxic chemicals.

• All the play corners in this book use 38mm x 19mm timber battens to form the framework. Connections between battens use screw fixings.

• Batten to batten fixings can be joined by 32mm dry-wall, self-tapping screws. These screws are easily driven home and can be used without having to drill a pilot hole.

• In most situations, corrugated cardboard will be adequate for forming panels and can usually be obtained at little cost.

• Hardboard is a flexible, cheap and splinter-free material to use for forming panels, particularly where they can expect wear. However, hardboard does not readily accept staples from a staple gun, so where a large amount of stapling is required plywood should be considered.

• Screw fixings to walls can be made using plugs with screws in the normal way, but ensure that no pipes or wires lie behind the wall you are fixing to. Screws can easily be removed when the play corner has to be dismantled.

• Galvanised wire netting (chicken-wire) is ideal for forming non-geometric shapes and can be stapled to timber framing if more sturdy support is required. Care should be taken to conceal the cut edges of the wire.

Additional play corner themes

Shops: village shop; supermarket; shoe shop; clothes shop; haberdasher's; greengrocer's; butcher's

Homes: flat; bungalow; bedsit; holiday chalet

Homes of other lands: tepee; igloo; mud hut

Historical themes: a Victorian kitchen; a Victorian schoolroom; an air raid shelter; an Aztec temple; Guy Fawkes' cellar; Noah's ark; a dinosaur's den

Services: library; carpenter's workshop; gymnasium; fire station; police station; hospital; dentist's surgery; doctor's surgery; health clinic; estate agent's office; theatres; banks; photographer's studio; weather station; telephone exchange; recording studio

Imaginary places: fairyland palace; castles; dungeons; magic grotto; outer space

Transport: bus; car; bus station; airport; railway station; train; submarine; Postman Pat's van; Noah's ark; ambulance; police car; taxi

Places we visit: the local park; an amusement/theme park; a fairground; a farm

Theme corners based on a book: Charlie's chocolate factory; Hansel and Gretel's cottage; the three bears' house; Treasure island; the Hobbit's cave; Charlotte's web; Kipper's kennel; Frog and Toad's home; Mr Thin's house

Miscellaneous: artist's studio; headteacher's office; school office (administration); staffroom; professor's laboratory; inventor's room; inside a whale; in the air; churches; temples; greenhouse; garden shed; lighthouse; stable; toy workshop; factory

Details of picture books listed on pages 72 and 73:

Percy the Park Keeper by Nick Butterworth (Collins 1997)
Can't You Sleep, Little Bear? by Martin Waddell and Barbara Firth (Walker 1988)
Whatever Next by Jill Murphy (Macmillan 1995)
The Lighthouse Keeper's Lunch by Ronda and David Armitage (Scholastic 1977)

The Queen's Knickers by Nicholas Allan (Red Fox 1995)
Funnybones by Allan Ahlberg and André Amstutz (Mammoth 1991)
Elmer by David McKee (Red Fox 1997)
Ruby by Maggie Glenn (Red Fox 1992)
Pingu (BBC Children's Books 1995)

Dedication

This book is dedicated to my dad, who has been my lifelong inspiration, and to my mum for her endless support and encouragement

---

Acknowledgements

I would like to thank all the staff at Westlea Primary School, Swindon, Wiltshire, without whom this book would not have happened, and particularly Ray Rogers, our caretaker, whose design and construction skills inspired us all.

Special thanks are due to:
Christine Adams, Yvonne Adams, Sue Anderson, Sue Axon Eaves, Rachel Badman, Judith Blake, Dale Burr, Bev Cable, Moira Calas, Stephanie Evans, Jan Griffin, Stuart Hall, Marilyn Harrison, Paula Kimber, Judith Kitson, Bridget Long, Gwen Metcalfe, Liz New, Anne Onslow, Jo McCombe, Peter Newbury, Alison Pass, Jan Preston, Suzanne Seaton, Sue Sheikh, Sheryl Staton, Mandy Sturman, Kathy Taylor, Julia Thompson, Jan Trevascus, Anne Wang, Liz Wood, Pam Woollard and Gill Young for their creativity and commitment to learning through play.

And thanks also to:
Selina Phillips (Christchurch Primary School, Bradford-on-Avon), Ruth Scholes (Penhill Infant School, Swindon), Sara Coulter (Brookfield Primary School, Swindon), Scott Mann, Sylvia Wright, Anne Pratt and Joan Jarvis for their contributions.

First published in 1998 by:
Stanley Thornes (Publishers) Ltd
Ellenborough House
Wellington Street
CHELTENHAM GL50 1YW
England

98 99 00 01 02/ 10 9 8 7 6 5 4 3 2 1

A catalogue record for this book is available from the British Library
ISBN 0-7487-3087-7

Typeset by Aetos Ltd. Bathampton, Bath.
Illustrations by Aetos Ltd. Bathampton, Bath.
Printed and bound in China by Dah Hua Printing Co.